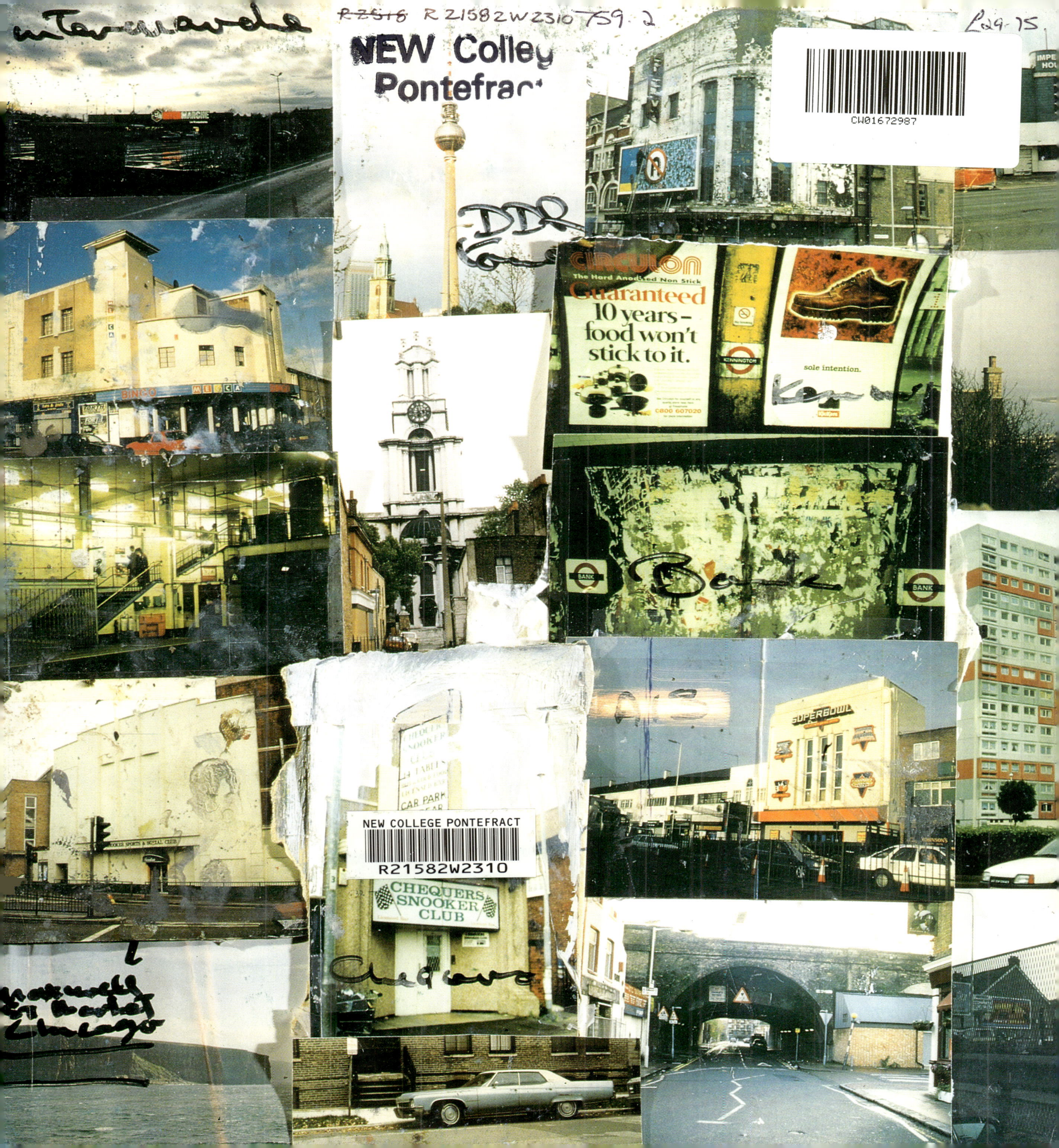

NEW College
Pontefract
R21582W2310 759.2
£29.95
CW01672987
NEW COLLEGE PONTEFRACT
R21582W2310

Jock McFadyen A Book About a Painter

by David Cohen

with

Lewis Biggs

Humphrey Ocean

Howard Jacobson

Bob and Roberta Smith

Hugo Williams

Tom Lubbock

Ian Dury

Mary Rose Beaumont

Duncan Macmillan

Jeffery Camp

Will Self

Lund Humphries

First published in 2001 by
Lund Humphries
Gower House
Croft Road
Aldershot
Hampshire GU11 3HR

Lund Humphries is part of Ashgate Publishing

Jock McFadyen: A Book About a Painter Copyright © Jock McFadyen and Susie Honeyman
Text Copyright © 2001 The Authors

British Library Cataloguing-in-Publication Data
A catalogue record for this book is available from the British Library

ISBN 0 85331 791 7

All rights reserved. No part of this publication may be reproduced, stored in a retrieval system or transmitted in any form or by any means, electrical, mechanical or otherwise, without first seeking the permission of the copyright owners and the publishers.

Library of Congress Card Number: 00-110810

Designed by Ray Carpenter
Typeset by Tom Knott
Printed in Singapore under the supervision of MRM Graphics

Ashgate US office:
Ashgate Publishing Company
131 Main Street
Burlington
VT 05401
USA

Distributed to the book trade in North America by
Antique Collectors' Club
Market Street Industrial Park
Wappingers Falls
NY 12590
USA

PAGE 4
Looking out to sea I, (detail) 1996
oil on canvas, 173 x 122 cm

PAGES 6,7
Turners Road after the Great Storm, 1987

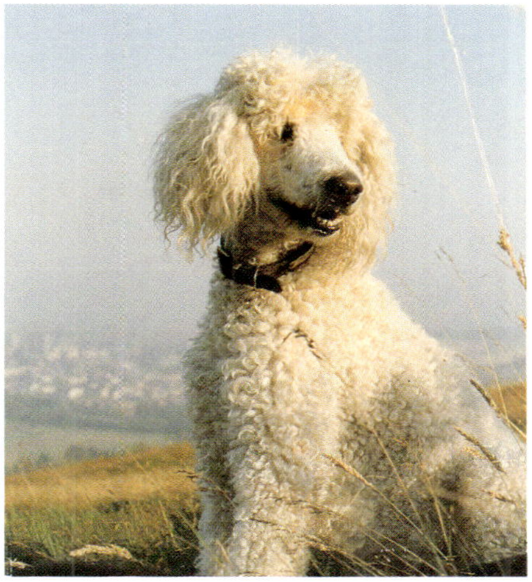

Acknowledgements

This book has been generously supported by The Arts Council of England and The Elephant Trust.

Many thanks to Jonathan Blond and William Jackson for their invaluable help with archive material, to Lucy Clark, Lucy Myers and Elfriede Windsor at Lund Humphries, and to Ray Carpenter for his design. Thanks also to Mary Rose Beaumont, Lewis Biggs, Jeffery Camp, Howard Jacobson, Tom Lubbock, Duncan Macmillan, Humphrey Ocean, Will Self, Bob and Roberta Smith and Hugo Williams for their contributions, and to Sophy Dury for the use of *Billericay Dickie*. James Atlee, Andrew King, Jonathan Moberly, Per and Parvati Sandven, John Taylor and Jo Walton have also helped with the project. Much gratitude is due to David Cohen for his work on the main text, and to Susie Honeyman for all her work on the book and for having the idea to make it in the first place.

Photographic credits

The artist and the publisher would like to acknowledge the following photographers for their work.

David Brown
Bill Cooper
Prudence Cuming
David Fiddeman
Adrian Harris
Susie Honeyman
Belinda Larmour
Jock McDougall
David McFadyen
Colin Mills
Gerard Mitchell
Duncan Poundcake
Liz Rideal
Rodney Todd-White & Son
Gareth Winters

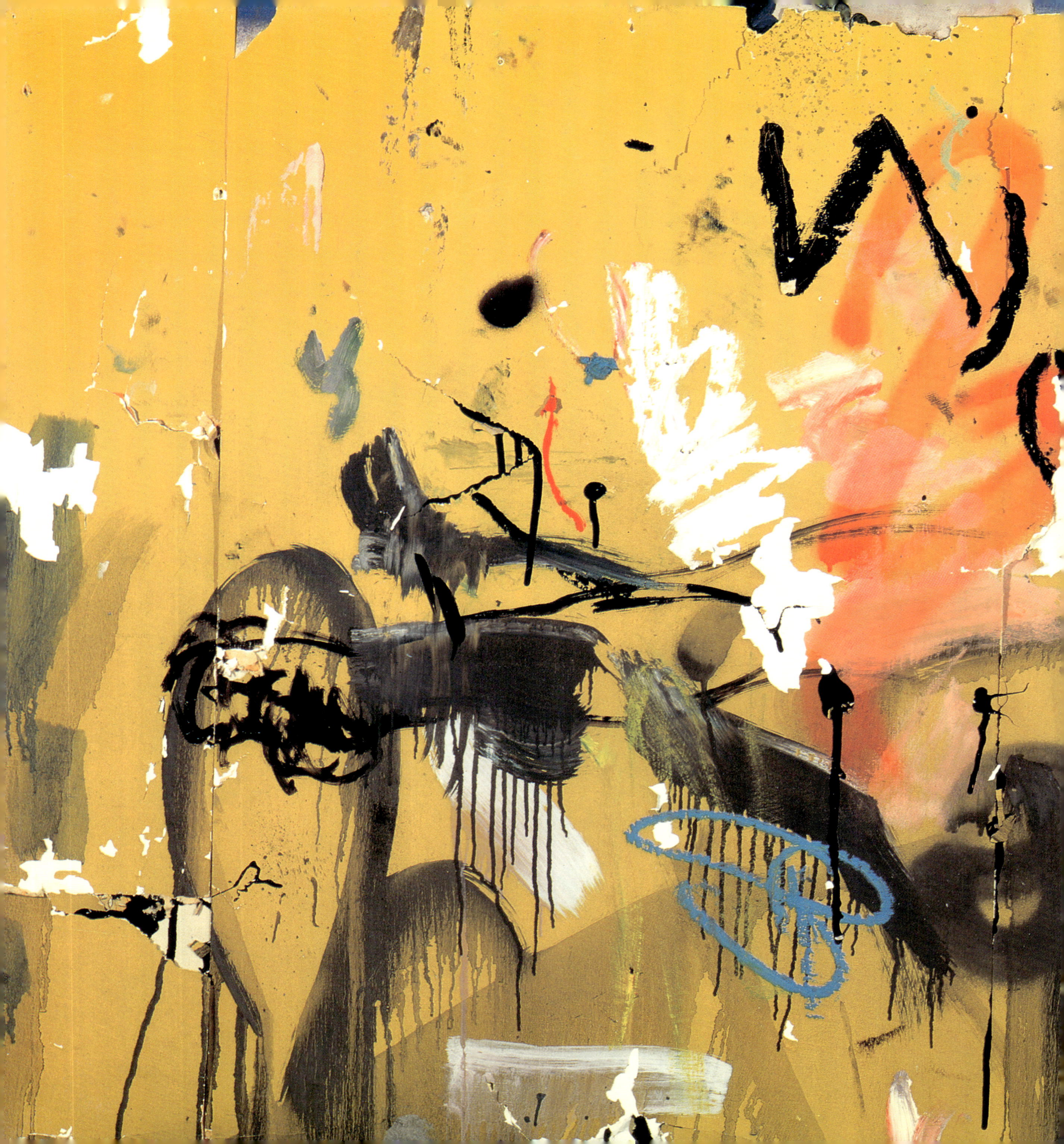

For Susie

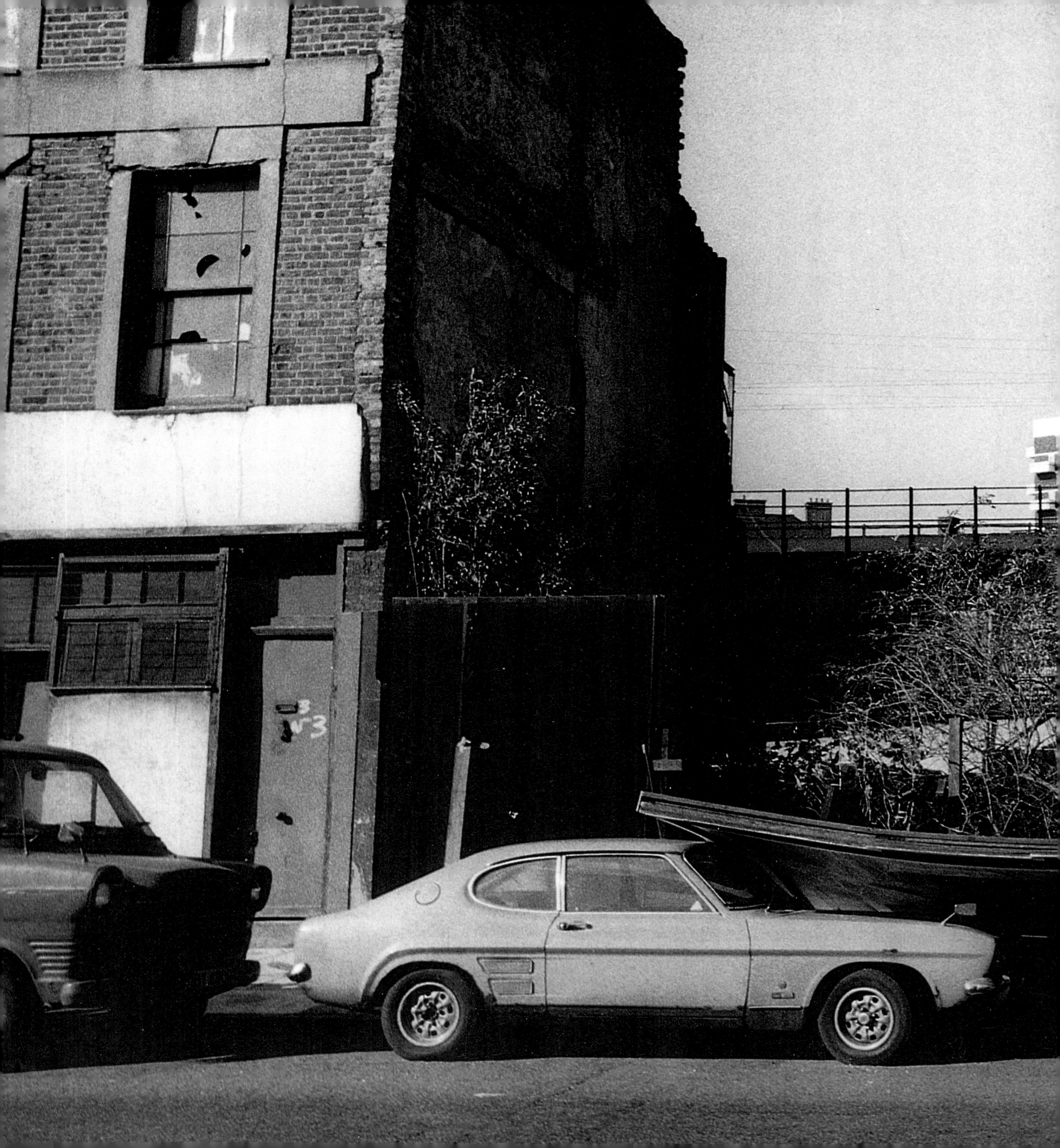

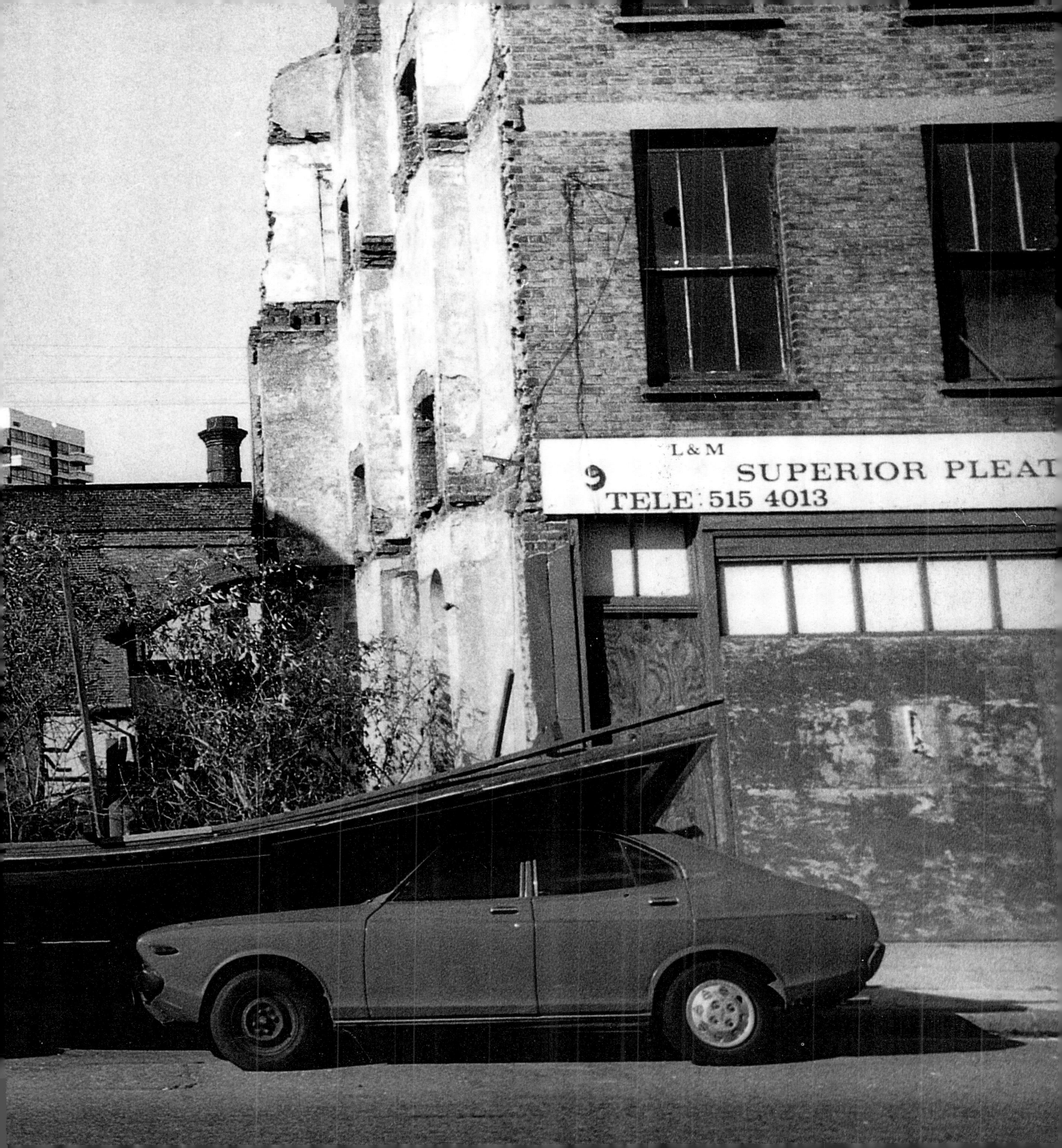
L & M
SUPERIOR PLEAT
TELE: 515 4013

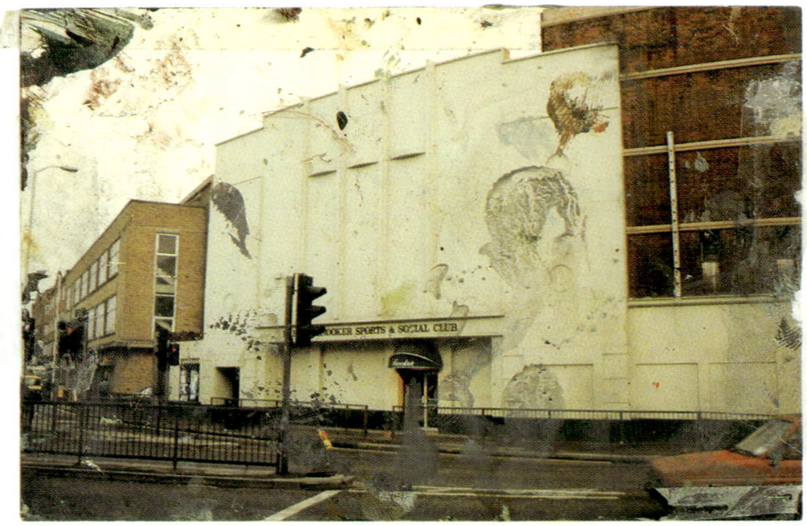
SPORTS & SOCIAL CLUB

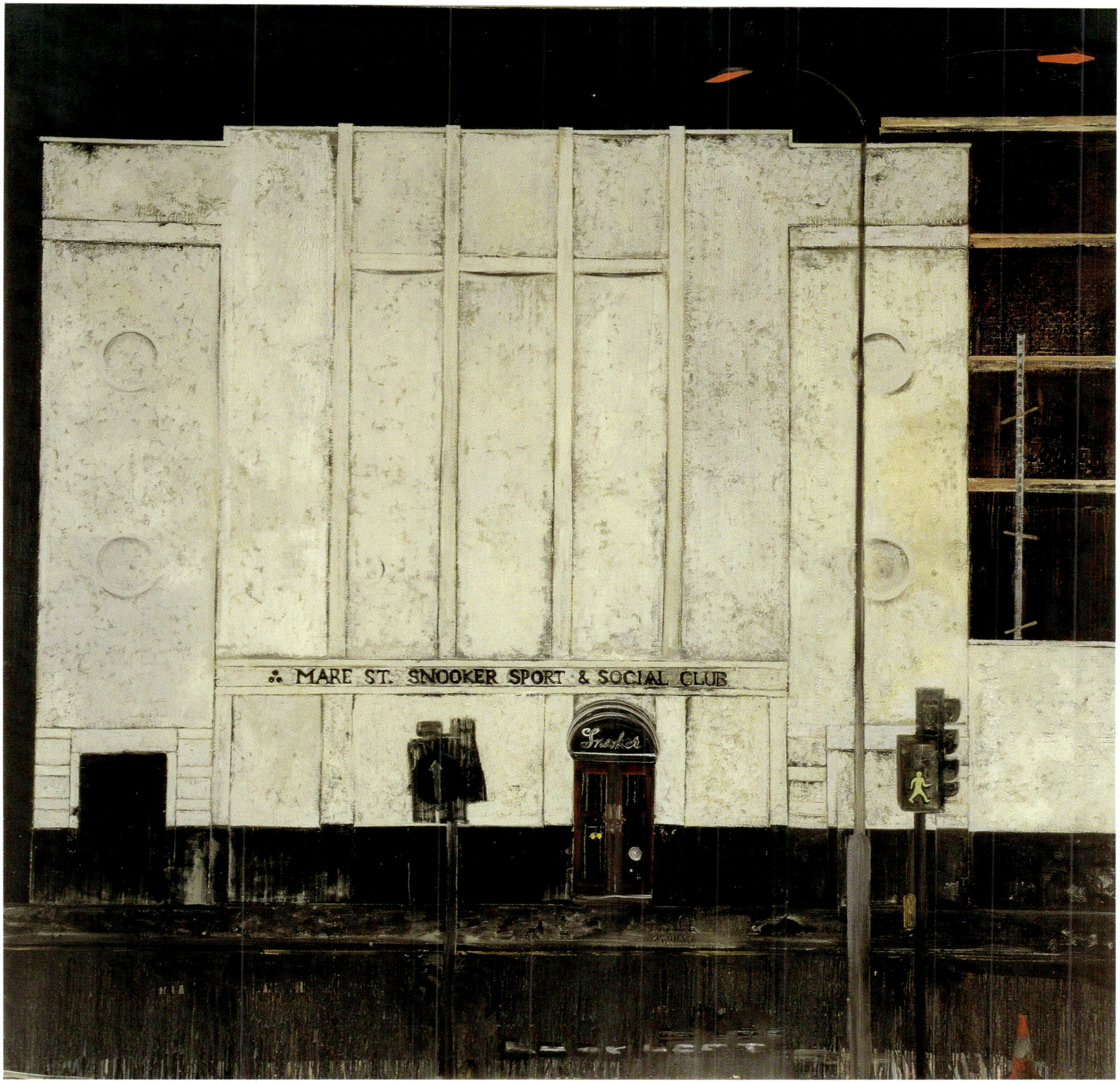

Mare Street Snooker Centre, 1994, oil on canvas, 203 x 203 cm

Jock McFadyen: A Painter's Progress

Jock McFadyen: A Painter's Progress

JOCK MCFADYEN is a maverick: his art is plucky and idiosyncratic, and eschews easy categorising. He exploits cartoon-like features without degrading his images to mere caricature. His people are extraordinary inventions, but are not bereft of individuality. He captures telling situations without resorting to illustration. He follows an obsession with observational detail without losing the vital sap that gives his images their unmistakable edge. And he has the balls to work in a national tradition without making art that is parochial or polite.

But being a maverick does not place McFadyen outside the critical discourse of his time. Part of his pluck, it could be argued, is to be himself and yet make himself relevant to what has been happening around him. Indeed, his relationship to the art world is exactly the same as his relationship to the historical times: aware, but not subservient. He has compassion and respect for the marginalised within society, and a shrewd idea of how they got there, but has never needed to make propaganda for some political cause. Similarly, he has an eye on the big issues of art, both current and perennial – the opposition between artifice and reality, between personal and neutral vision; the relevance of painting in an age dominated by photography; the question of national versus international style – without needing to make art which is 'about art' to prove that awareness. Current concerns are not so much reflected in his art as absorbed into it.

McFadyen is passionately devoted to the northern English realist L.S. Lowry (1887–1976), who towards the end of his life became popular for his quirky depictions of the industrial landscape, but was for the most part dismissed by the art world of his day. McFadyen points with astonishment to the near-abstract seascapes that Lowry often painted – pale, almost monochromatic canvases consisting of a simple horizon line and the slightest intimations of waves. 'He is not Barnett Newman but a product of a local arts club. It is a testament to his vision, up in Salford. It is heroic that he was able to do this. He is totally underrated – no one has attended to his ability to be a modernist *and* an outsider.'[1]

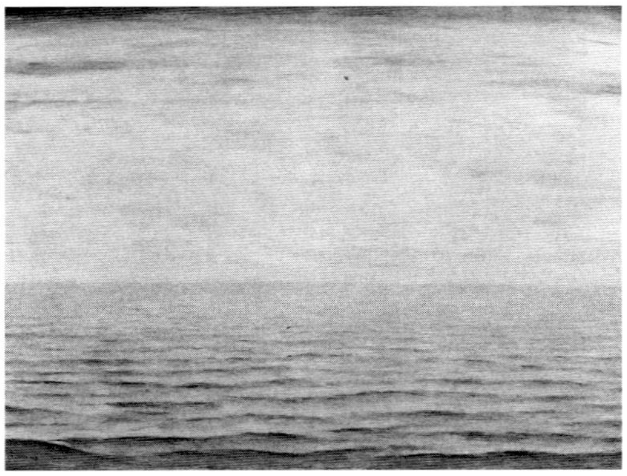

The Sea, L.S. Lowry, 1965
City of Salford Museums and Art Gallery
© Lowry Estate

1. Unless otherwise noted, quotations from the artist are taken from conversations with the author in 1999 and 2000.

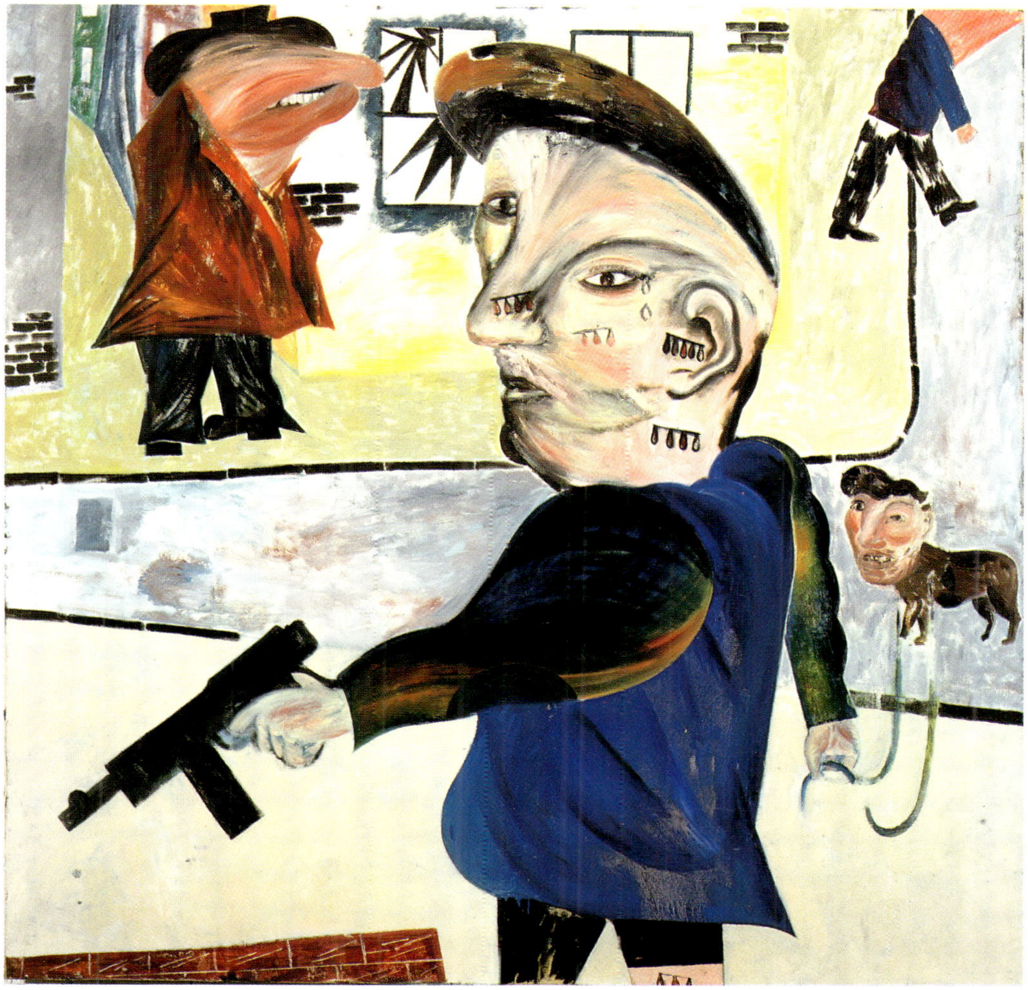

The Street, 1980, oil on canvas, 173 x 173 cm

It would be absurd to claim of McFadyen, who has studied at Chelsea, has an MA, and has taught for many years for one day a week at the Slade, that he is an outsider, but in this way of expressing admiration for Lowry there is some degree of self-reflection. Lowry and McFadyen are linked by a struggle shared by every serious artist: to be alive to the active possibilities in the art of one's times and yet remain true to an inner vision.

•

Jock McFadyen was born in 1950, and it is perhaps this synchronicity with the century that inclines him to think, neatly, in decades. There have been two significant about-turns in his career that he himself is aware of, and these occurred at the outset of the 1980s and 1990s, respectively. In the first instance, his residency at London's National Gallery, in 1980–1, forced a major reconsideration of where he was taking his art. He had been exhibiting since he graduated from Chelsea in 1977; he had been in the John Moore's, the prestigious open exhibition of emerging painters held biennially in Liverpool; he was with the upcoming dealer Jonathan Blond, had a fulsome Arts Council grant in 1979, and generally seemed 'well set' with the jokey, cartoon-like images that brought him the honour of being the second artist in residence at the National Gallery (following Maggi Hambling, who is five years his senior). Although he made a point of not copying works in the Gallery collections during his time there – adopting, by his own account, a 'bolshy' stance at his interview, he said that he would represent 'living' art – proximity to the Old Masters led to something of a turning point. The appropriationist, synthetic art-about-art that had characterised his practice until then seemed somewhat lacking; he realised this project was not big enough for a life's work. With the advent of the Falklands War in 1982, a political instinct came to confirm this view. 'The sense of desolation mixed with jingoism on the street seemed a much bigger subject than the option of playing postmodernist games with the graphics of war', he says, referring to the new computer graphics on TV which he realised would have fascinated him more in his semiotic days. Self-consciously, he put a 'schematic' kind of picture-making behind him, and set about making art rooted in observation: observation, that is, in both the social and visual sense.

The second epiphany occurred a decade later, in 1991–2, when he was at work on a major commission to design a ballet for Sir Kenneth MacMillan – the great choreographer's last piece, as it turned out. The characters, costumes and setting for *The Judas Tree* were based on McFadyen paintings such as *Costa del Dogs*: ballerina Viviana Durante ended up in a stripy dress just like the East End dame of this particular picture. Ironically, though, the translation of McFadyen's painted figures to dancers on the stage served to 'debrief' him as a figure painter. Working on the 'flats' for this production he found himself fully absorbed in the depiction of buildings; it was a cathartic experience. As a solitary painter in his studio, McFadyen says, he liked to paint figures to keep himself company. The experience of collaboration with a ballet company freed him up to do without them.

This is the armature of McFadyen's career so far, then: art school and schematic images in the 1970s; the National Gallery and observed figure compositions in the 1980s; the Royal Ballet, cityscapes and landscapes in the 1990s. However, the competing tendencies towards the schematic and the observed, towards figure and environment, are not exclusively resolved at each change of direction. Instead, the opposition is sometimes to be found active within an individual image.

Consider, for instance, a painting from the mid-point of McFadyen's career: *Copperfield Road* (1990). It has many of the ingredients that epitomise the artist's singular world view. The lived-in woman's face is brutal and defiant; with its strange contours it is rather sci-fi like but at the same time lovably real, like W.H. Auden's face with its trademark wrinkles. Aspects of the generic and the particular cohabit within her features. Just as this woman is both archetypal and actual,

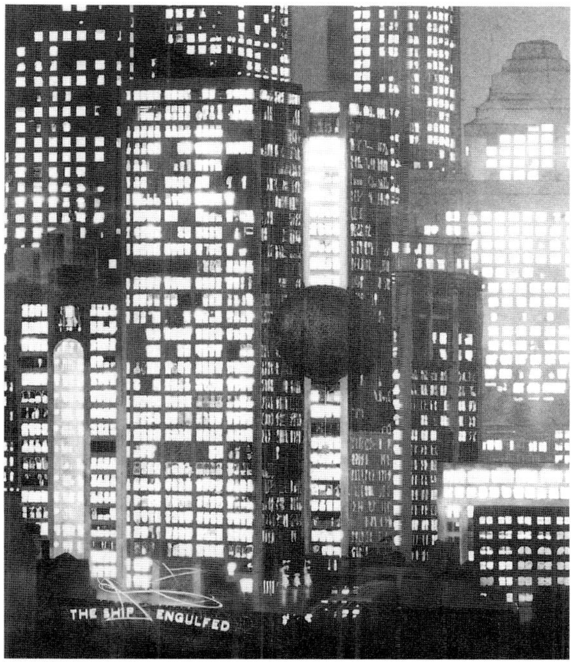

Lights II: The Ship Engulfed, Michael Andrews, 1972
Arts Council Collection, Hayward Gallery, London
© Artist's Estate

so, too, is Copperfield Road akin to the metaphoric 'wasteland' and yet a topographically credible slice of London life. The dogs are generalised in a cartoonish way, but no less craftily observed for that. There is squalor and decay, but also a sense of nature claiming back the artifice of human habitation. The graffiti creeping in at the side – transforming the city into the jungle – finds equivalence in the blades of grass, the latter drawn in with the obsessional, slightly nutty fastidiousness of certain graffiti writers. There is no neat resolution of the schematic-versus-observational dichotomy. However, rather than, with historic hindsight, viewing *Copperfield Road* as a 'transitional' work, it is more liberating to see within the image a kind of yin–yang, push–pull opposition that energises it and compels our attention towards it all the more.

•

Jock McFadyen is a figurative painter who was taught by non-figurative artists. Obduracy and personal vision attach him to a legacy that is usually passed on, baton-like, from teacher to pupil. His heroes in modern British art include individuals such as Walter Sickert and Michael Andrews – we will see the extent of their influence later on, in the 1990s. From Sickert it is possible to draw 'family trees'. Sickert was a mentor to David Bomberg, who taught, at evening classes, Frank Auerbach and Leon Kossoff. The men who formed the Euston Road School in the 1930s, meanwhile considered themselves protégés of Sickert, too. William Coldstream went on to direct the Slade, where star pupils in the 1950s included Euan Uglow and Michael Andrews. None of this genealogy should diminish the fact that realism is a tradition constantly ruptured and renewed. It is only as strong as its practitioners, who rebel against their instruction as often as they accept it. To understand McFadyen's style, however, is to delve into the mystery of an artist who broke rank with the perceived direction and orthodoxies of his day, whether abstract or conceptual, to be a realist, yet has retained more than might seem obvious from the people who taught him.

At the age of sixteen, McFadyen moved south of the border from his native Scotland with his family. He did his foundation year (the preparatory year before going to art college) at Newcastle-under-Lyme School of Art. The year was 1966, and art education in Britain was very much in the thrall of Basic Design, a modernist experiment with art training pioneered, amongst others, by Victor Pasmore and Richard Hamilton at the other Newcastle (Newcastle-upon-Tyne). At the time of McFadyen's studies, Basic Design began to gather force as the new orthodoxy. McFadyen, however, would have nothing to do with the fragmentary array of activities planned for the novice: he subjected himself to a solid year of life drawing, which his instructors considered passé. Eventually he was expelled without gaining the qualification he needed to continue his education. He spent the next five years at various jobs – he was even a dustman for a while. By 1972 he was married and had a son. The following year he enrolled at Chelsea School of Art from where he graduated with a BA in 1976 and an MA in 1977.

At Chelsea, he recalls, the majority of teachers tended towards abstraction – among them were figures such as Sean Scully, Stephen Buckley and Ian Stephenson – while fellow students were experimenting with land art, mail art and aspects of peformance and conceptualism. Stephenson's guidance was important to him, as was that of draughtsman Ron Bowen and film-maker Anne Rees-Mogg. McFadyen's peers included Helen Chadwick, Anish Kapoor and Alexi Sayle, who went on to be a comedian. McFadyen himself was most influenced at this time by Pop Art. The teaching staff was abstract-heavy, he now reasons, 'because the Pop artists were selling so well they didn't need to teach!'. The prevailing mood in the school was that Pop had had its day, whereas colour field painting, although rooted in an earlier practice, still had *gravitas*.

If McFadyen was pursuing an artistic course that went against the grain, it was a far from melancholy one. Idiosyncratic and full of high jinks, his highly eclectic and appropriationist work of this period referenced a variety of styles. In particular he looked very closely at the British Pop artists who had risen to ascendancy in the 1960s, especially the group that had graduated from the Royal College at the start of that decade, among them R.B. Kitaj, David Hockney and Allen Jones. (Jones, incidentally, has the distinction of being the first collector of

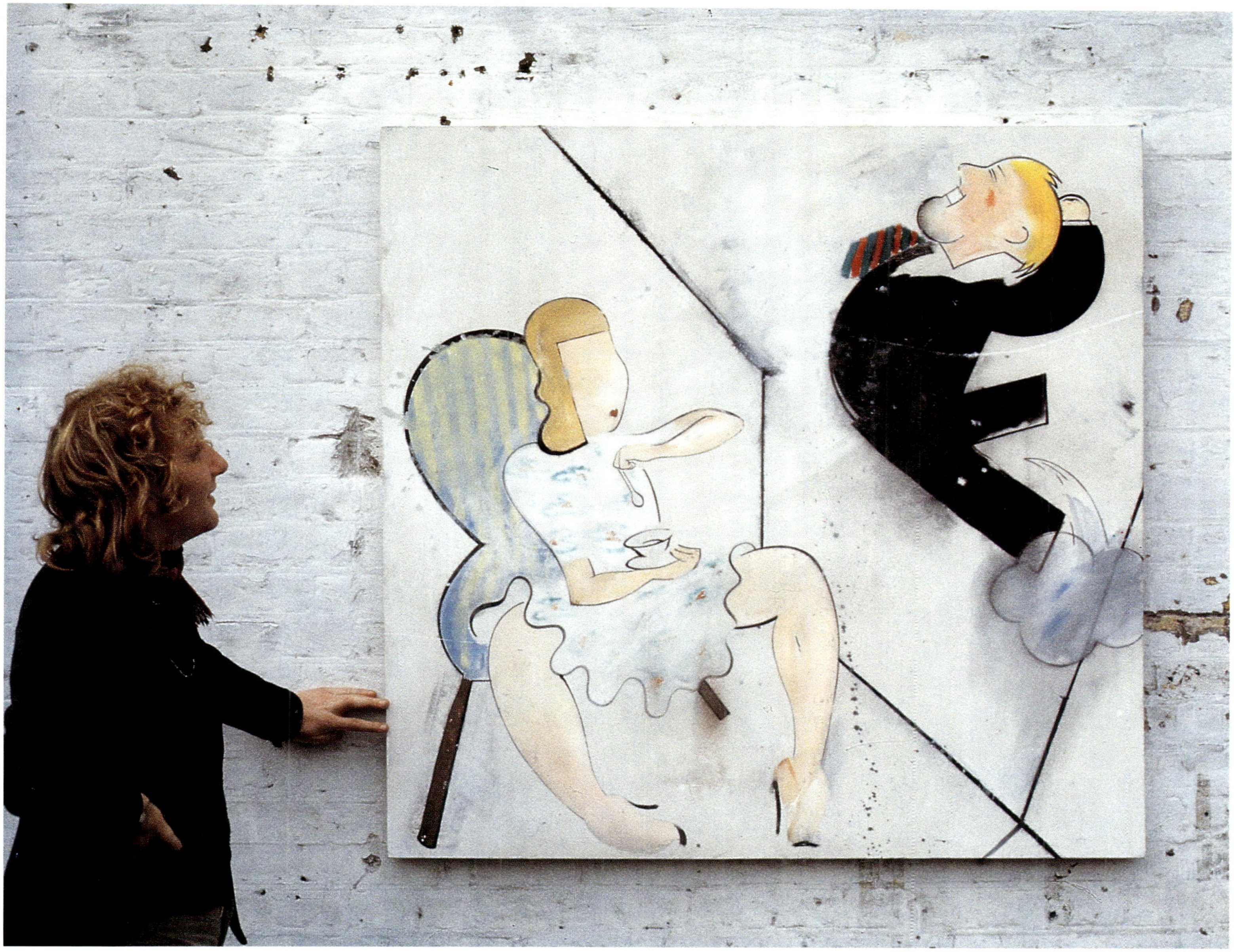

Jock McFadyen and the painting *Those heady days, seemed to last forever, Siegfried jumping around like the big idiot he was* (Arts Council Collection) Butlers Wharf, 1978

McFadyen's work, having bought a piece from a student show.) The dominatrix at the centre of McFadyen's 1978 drawing *Those heady days, seemed to last forever, Siegfried jumping around like the big idiot he was*, with her voluptuous, nonchalantly extended leg and loosened (or is it tortuously contorted?) high-heeled shoe, might be a distant cousin of the fetish-gear-clad women who stalk Jones's canvases. There is an affinity with early Kitaj, too, in the exalted, flattened-out block-figure male – no doubt the Siegfried of the convoluted title (another Kitaj-like trait). But the image looks further afield, taking in something of El Lissitzky's exuberant Constructivist children's illustrations.

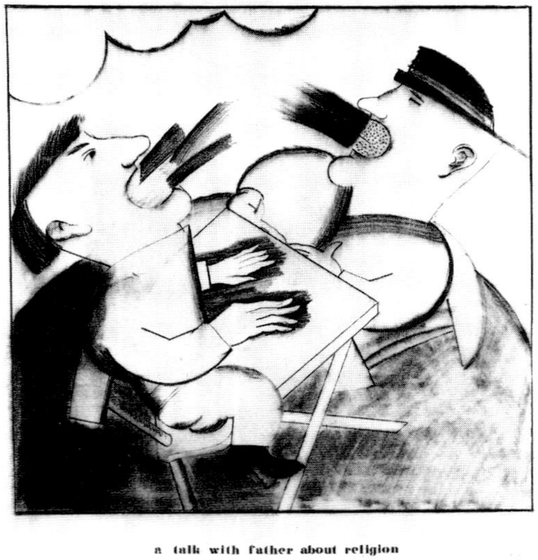

A talk with father about religion, 1978
pencil on paper, 76 x 56 cm, Private collection

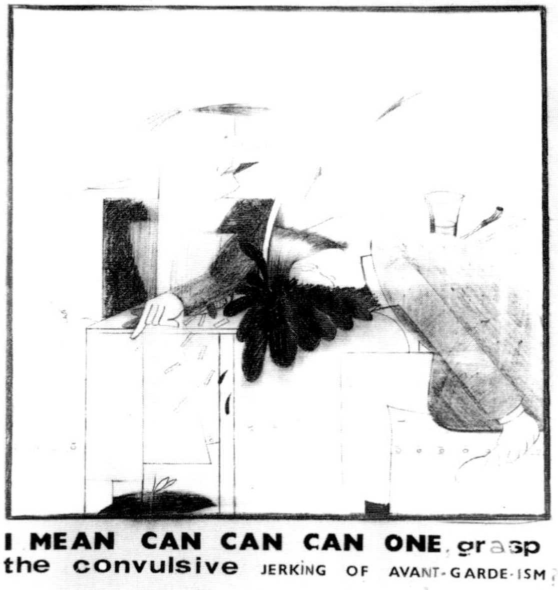

I mean can can can one grasp the convulsive jerking of avant-garde-ism? 'Absolutely', 1978,
pencil on paper, 76 x 56 cm, Private collection

A more enduring influence for this self-consciously 'northern' artist was early twentieth-century German art, including both the Expressionists and the Neue Sachlichkeit ('New Objectivity') realists of the Weimar Republic. *A talk with father about religion*, 1978, for instance, has the gutsy, grainy texture and tightness of George Grosz or Otto Dix. Father's cap is much like the First World War head-wear of the German and Austrian armies that is so familiar from Expressionist works. Both this image and *Siegfried* were included in McFadyen's second solo exhibition, held at the New 57 Gallery in Edinburgh in 1978. Tellingly, the show was billed as 'Paintings Drawings Titles', so as to emphasise that the titles inscribed underneath – or sometimes within – the images were to be treated with the same aesthetic consideration as the images themselves. The typography of these titles is often knowingly historicised.

•

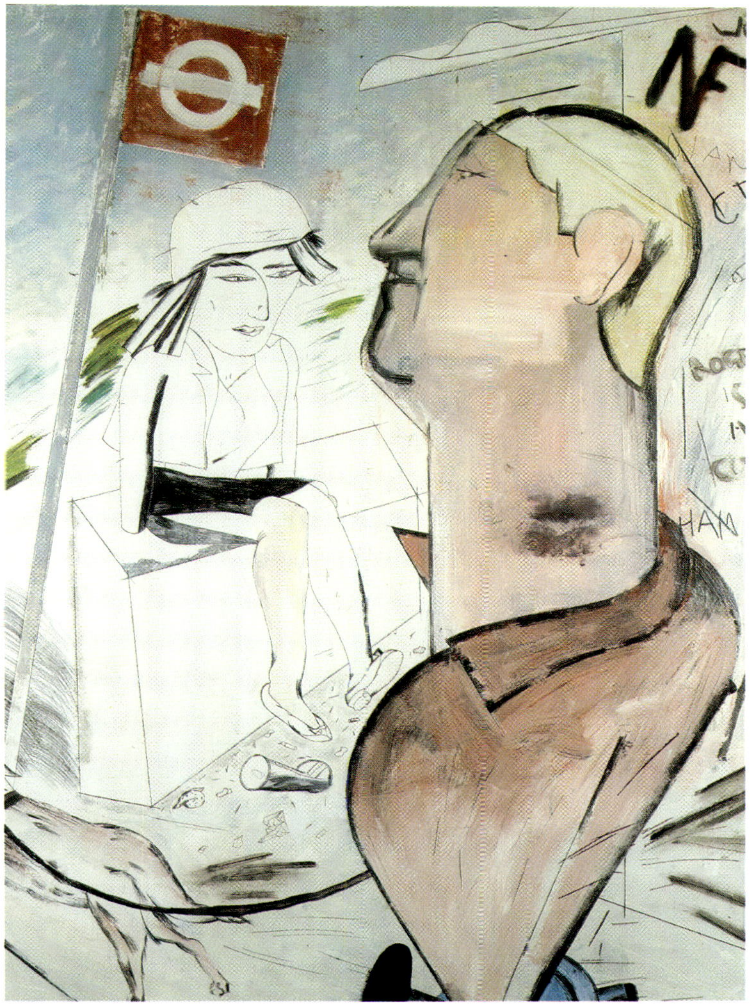

At the bus stop: the love bite, 1981, oil on card, 137 x 102 cm
The Victoria & Albert Museum, London

Most people can undergo a spiritual conversion but still look pretty much the same person, but an artistic conversion should demonstrate tangible changes in the individual's work. McFadyen's *At the bus stop: the love bite*, 1981, exhibited at the National Gallery alongside other works made during his residency there, is, by the standards of observational realism he subsequently evolved, still pretty 'schematic'. There is no fundamental break with the cartoon-like language: witness the way the man's torso disappears, Popeye-style, into a foreshortened waist, from where it diminishes with even further exaggeration into minute buttocks and feet; the way his neck protrudes as a massive, rigid column; the bus stop that leans into the picture space; or the perspectival naivety of the sandbox upon which the girl is suggestively perched. What lifts this work out of 'schemata' and into the orbit of observation is not so much the means of rendering, as the attitude towards the real. The love bite that transforms – sensitises – the young blond proletarian with his contented smile, who might otherwise have walked his dog wearing a scowl as angry and violent as the Fascist graffiti on the wall, is a telling detail observed in life and magnified in art, rather than an element appropriated from other art or from the media and dropped knowingly into an image. 'It is this focus', Lewis Biggs has argued, 'this unmistakable but still mysterious element of true life story, which divides the new from the old.'[2] There are clues here that tell of a humanising visual acuity. The lover is depicted as though in technicolour, against the schematic black-and-white of his surroundings. The painterly is set up as a moral contrast to the graphic, as surely as the sign (London Transport) is an orderly opposition to the scrawl (NF, West Ham).

To see McFadyen's realism in terms of keeping opposites in balance is all well and good, but there is an alternative – and equally valid – view. This celebrates his ability to smash through a supposed opposition of the schematic and the observed (even though he subscribes to the distinction himself) to achieve a synthesis that is in tune with his own sense of the real. To be real his images need to be credible, rooted in observation, verifiable, factual. But they also need to be actual, which means felt, not measured; expressive, not referential. The pictorial conveyance has to have something of the energy of the first (primal, epiphanous) experience of seeing. Take the painting *Waiting for the Cortina boys*, from 1985. The road bends around the peninsula on which the two girls wait, and in so doing gathers up the barricade and subjects it to its own shape. This defies the laws of perspective but captures instead the girls' own perspective. There is a sensation of 'rush' as the paint thins out and the brushstrokes elongate, giving the sense of asphalt capturing light. This is at once painterly observation and a kind of naive identification on the painter's part with the energy of the scene he is making. We can almost imagine him making car noises as he paints the road. The road finds visual echo in the grass rushes at the foot of the composition, which in turn is playfully repeated in the brushed-off white graffiti marks on the brick wall. Sophisticated composition meets childlike perspective half-way in an adolescent fascination with detail: the brick-by-brick colouring of the wall, the minute messages and signatures on the girl's plaster of Paris, the trademarks on the Coke can, the Rothmans packet, the Budweiser bottle, the *Sun* newspaper. There is a whiff here of the Kitchen Sink School that prevailed in Britain in the 1950s, prefiguring Pop in its lavish attention to the realism of advertising and products. There, though unlike the Pop artists, this earlier group did not imbue their detritus with glamour, nor sentimental affection for its day to dayness – just an insistence on the real. McFadyen's car is obstinately specific, a Mark II Ford Cortina. We sense that McFadyen has looked for the right kind of wheel, and that it matters.

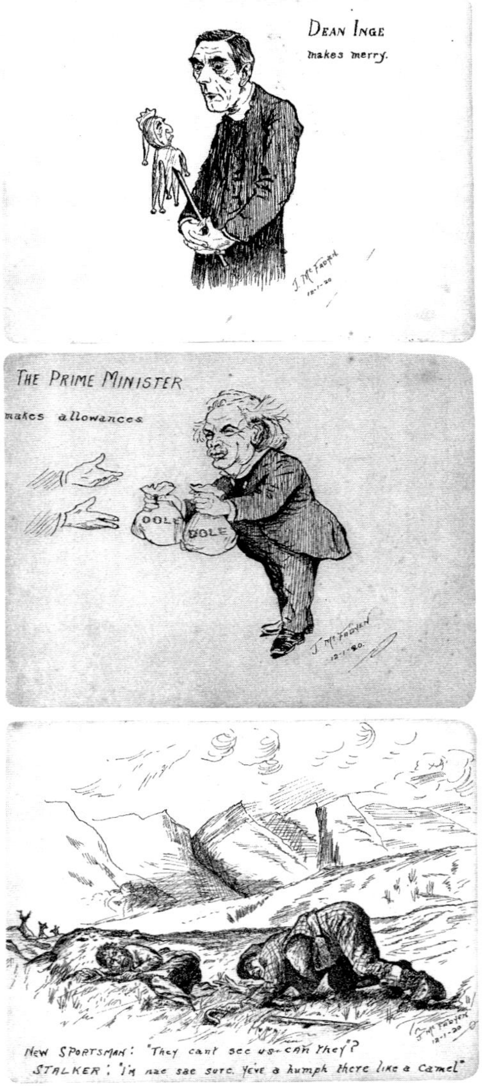

Satirical drawings, 1920, 12 x 16 cm, by James McFadyen, Jock McFadyen's grandfather

2. Lewis Biggs, 'Realism in Art, or a Slap in the Face with a Wet Kipper', in *Jock McFadyen: Paintings*, Sunderland, Northern Centre for Contemporary Art, 1986.

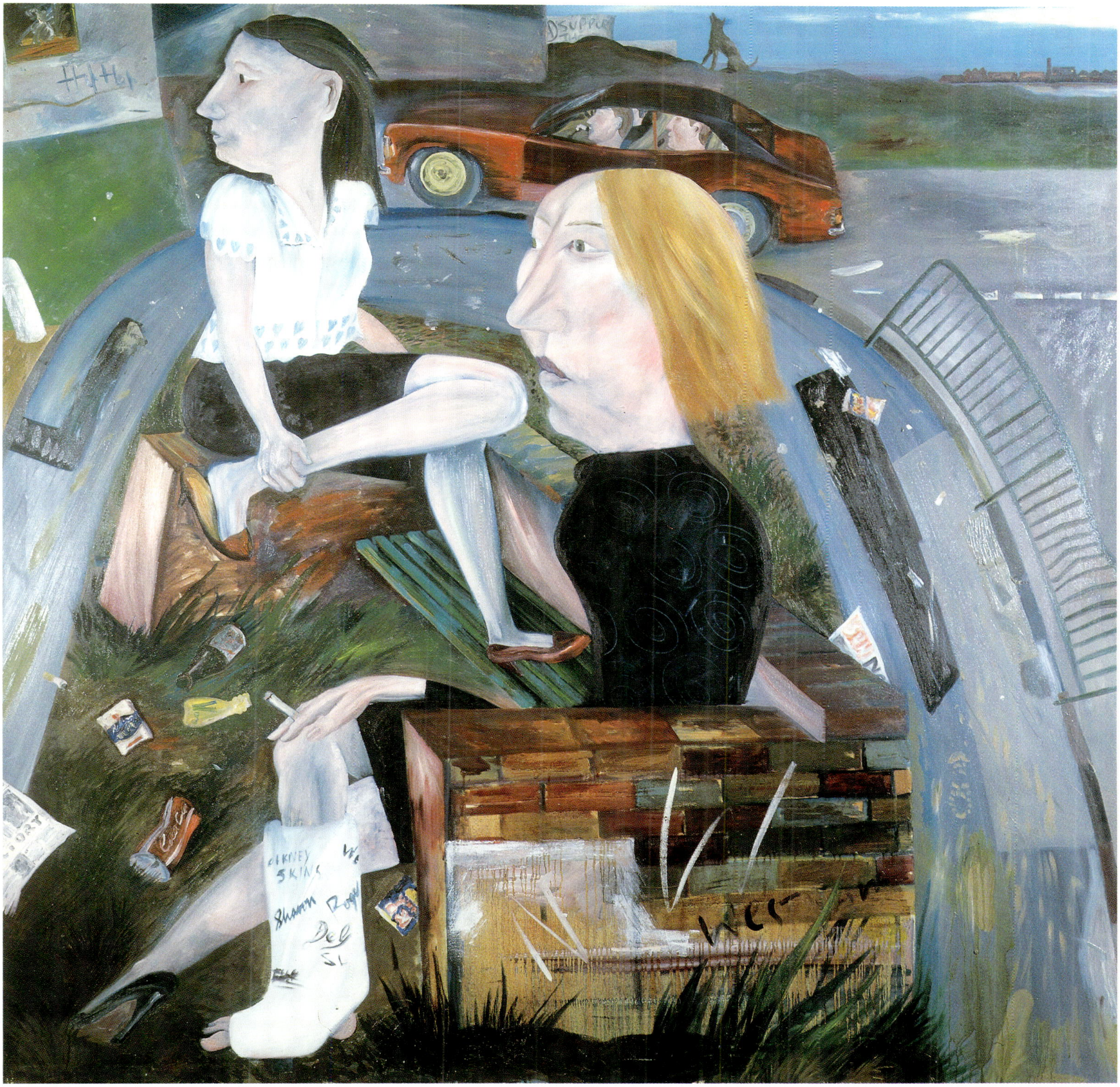

Waiting for the Cortina boys, 1985, oil on canvas, 213 × 213 cm, Manchester City Art Gallery

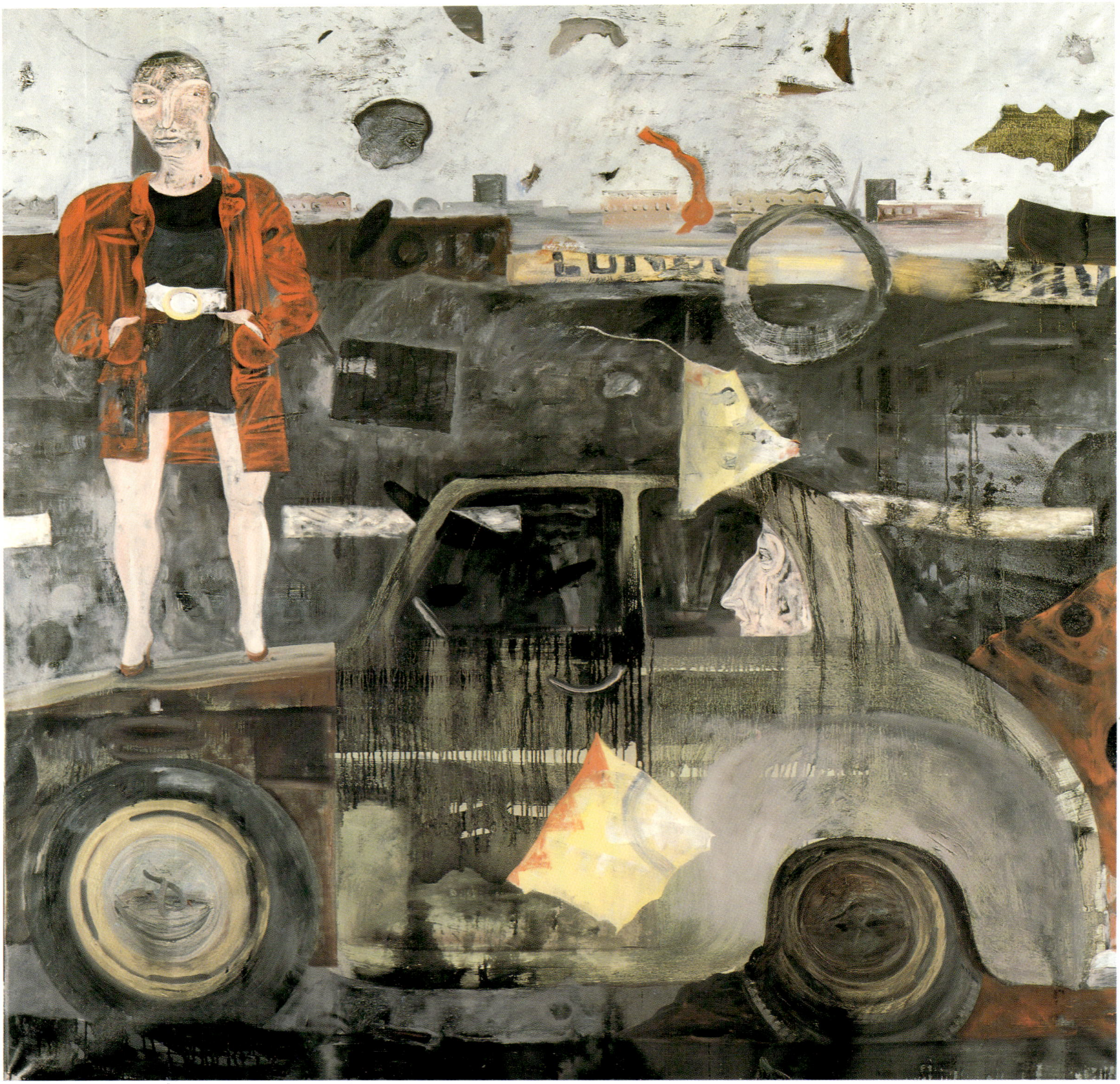

River at Wapping, 1989, oil on canvas, 203 x 203 cm

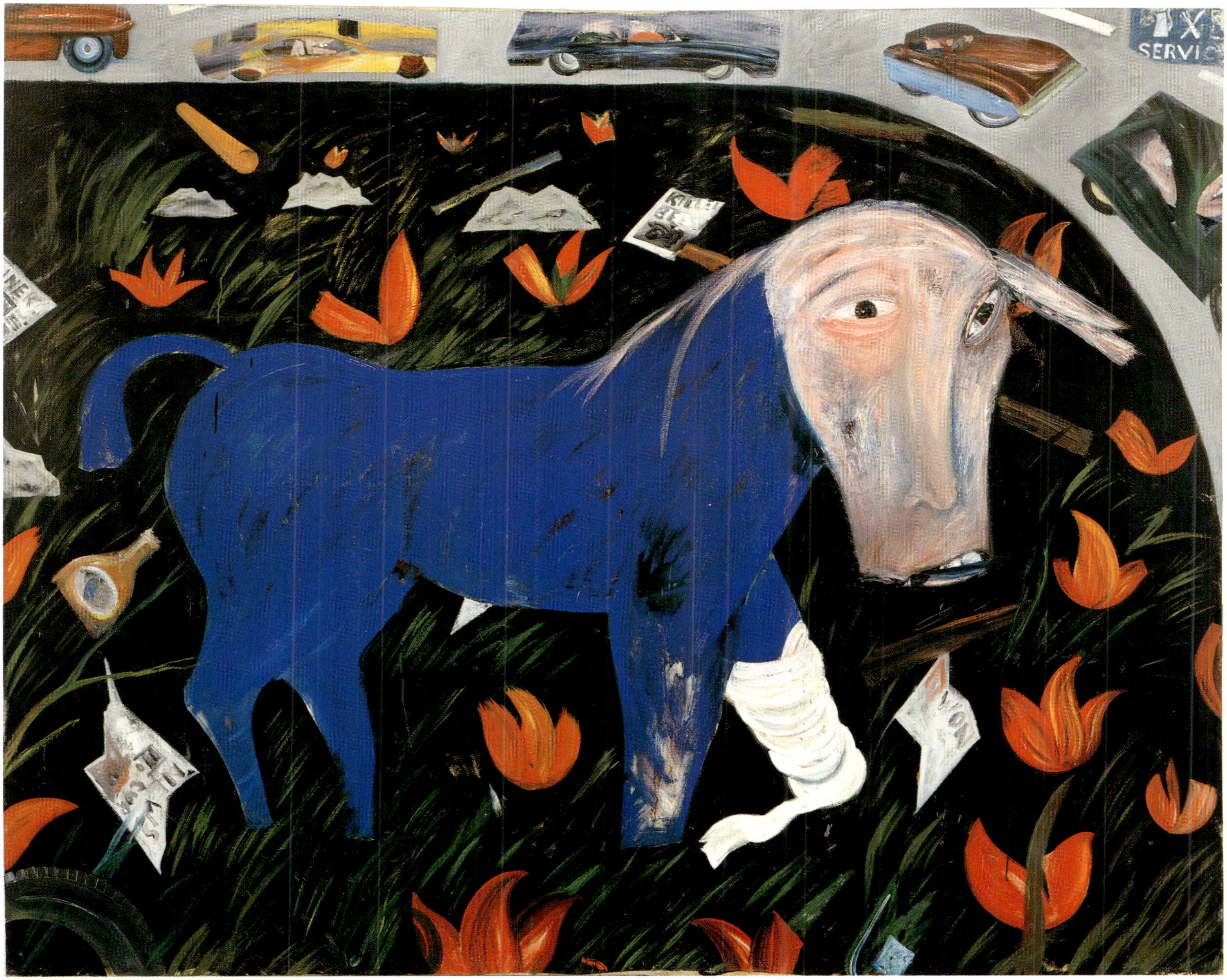

Horse lamenting the invention of the motor car, 1985
oil on canvas, 213 x 260 cm
Private collection

Horse lamenting the invention of the motor car, also from 1985, gives rise to the reflection that McFadyen is the Stubbs of the automobile: throughout his career cars have fascinated him. (He has even fabricated a sculptural monument to the fall of the Berlin Wall incorporating a burnt-out Trabant.) Perhaps this fascination is rooted in the artist's childhood, as his father, at that time a draughtsman in Glasgow's shipyards, taught him to draw cars as a boy. (His grandfather, incidentally, who also worked in the yards, was not only a gifted draughtsman but also an amateur political cartoonist.) McFadyen's horse laments the triumph of the mechanical over the organic, but the victory is shown to be pyrrhic: the artist's childlike rendering of cars gives them sinewy muscle in the body and bird-like eyes for windows as surely as his flattened-out horse is as sculptural and fabricated in the trunk as any horse of Uccello's. The choice of blue for the animal, as well as the anthropomorphism of its face, relates McFadyen to pioneers of ethereal other-worldliness in modern art such as Franz Marc and Marc Chagall. It underlines the fact that, as much as earthy, robust, empirical British realism might seem to pervade his world view, he is just as atuned to the traditions of magic realism. The strangely fragmentary *River at Wapping*, 1989 – another car image – recalls nothing so much as the closing pages of Gabriel García Márquez's *One Hundred Years of Solitude*, where the town that has been the setting of this novel suddenly, and inexplicably, internally combusts.

Magic aside, however, there is undoubtedly a gritty, grainy side to McFadyen's social vision. He conceives a uniquely British line of at once humorous and grotesque commentary that stretches back through Sickert and Lowry to Hogarth and Gillray, and forward to the macabre family photographs of Richard Billingham. He is fond of linking Sickert with the working-class TV soap opera 'Coronation Street' and the playwrights and directors Ken Loach, Mike Leigh and Alan Bleasdale, to underline his sensitivity towards the grubby and the prosaic in realism. In his images of urban decay and societal breakdown, there may not be a 'party line' as clear and emphatic as in his grandfather's socialist cartoons, nor is there unambiguous pity in his view of the dispossessed, but McFadyen's art is always imbued with a tender humanism. His humour does not give us licence to laugh at the poor; on the contrary, it lends these strange, sad people an almost heroic dignity. There may not be an obvious narrative at play in an image such as *Hawksmoor and Tesco*, 1988, but the scene inevitably brings to mind Hogarth and his ability to fuse the caricatural and the credible, the raucous and the edifying. This is Hogarth without the moral. There is nevertheless a hint of a message in the equation between Hawksmoor's church – to which the figures turn their backs, and which recedes on the horizon, its cross obscured in the branches – and the ubiquitous supermarket shopping bag, a shared symbol in the capitalist economy, which the old man grips with a clenched fist.

•

McFadyen's faces are as memorable as they are extraordinary. He has an uncanny ability to convey a sense of normality despite inflicting on faces a violence particular to his art. In this respect he bears comparison with Francis Bacon. On closer inspection, however, just as it seems we have worked out the essentials of the McFadyen face – accentuated sockets, striations like a Maori tattoo, wounds or disfigurements, and so on – it emerges that there is much greater painterly diversity in McFadyen's treatment of the face than Bacon's manner allows. The aggressive brushstrokes in *Three men and a dog*, 1985, giving an arched structure to each of the human faces, contrast with the much more dignified handling of

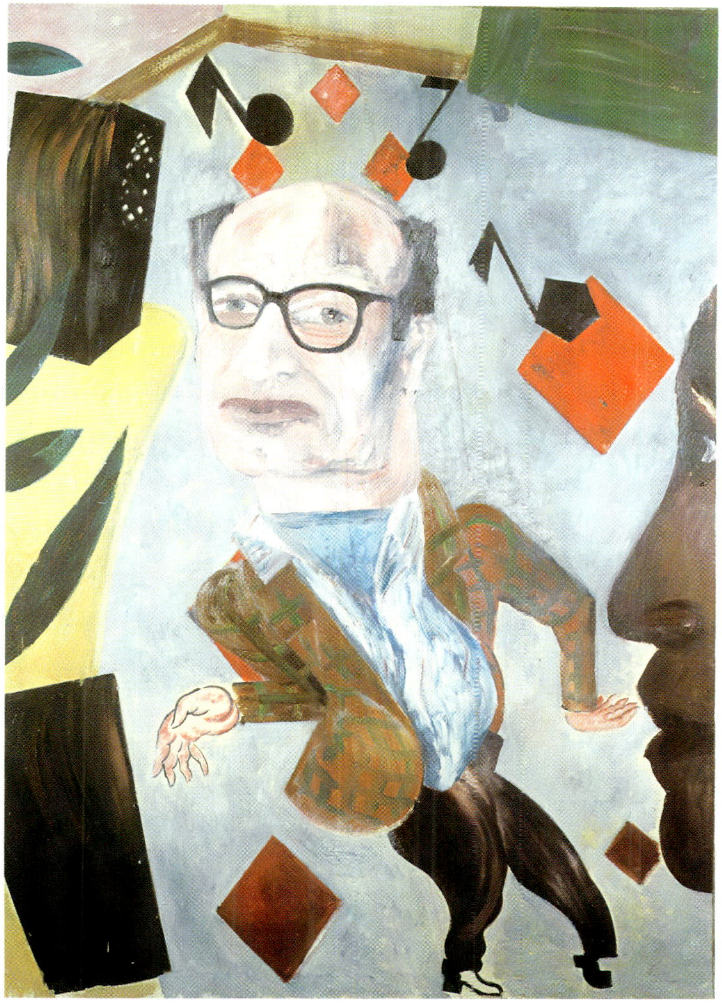

Harry Diamond dancing in Paul Tonkins' prefab, 1984
oil on canvas, 178 x 122 cm

Harry Diamond dancing in Paul Tonkins' prefab, 1984, which is perhaps more respectful for being a portrait of a named individual (Diamond, a significant photographer and character within the bohemian Soho scene of the 1950s, sat, on a couple of occasions, for Lucian Freud). Later in the decade McFadyen's faces – and figures – are much more caricatural, as in the case of the Asian women lined up to pay their electricity bills in *L.E.B*, 1989, or the snub-nosed man in *New York Subway*, 1988. Realism and surreal invention can cohabit the same canvas, as in *Two Prods on Sandy Row*, 1988, where the right-hand figure is conventionally straightforward, in contrast to his weird companion with the crater-like eye socket. By the turn of the next decade, when we are close to the end of McFadyen's active interest in the human figure, caricature and realism are melded in a technique that is particular to the artist, a recognisable personal style. The face leering out of *Canal*, 1991, is grotesque, but not absurd. It seems to belong to someone capable of terrible violence, and probably already the victim of it, too. It is as if the striations and

Text continues on page 32

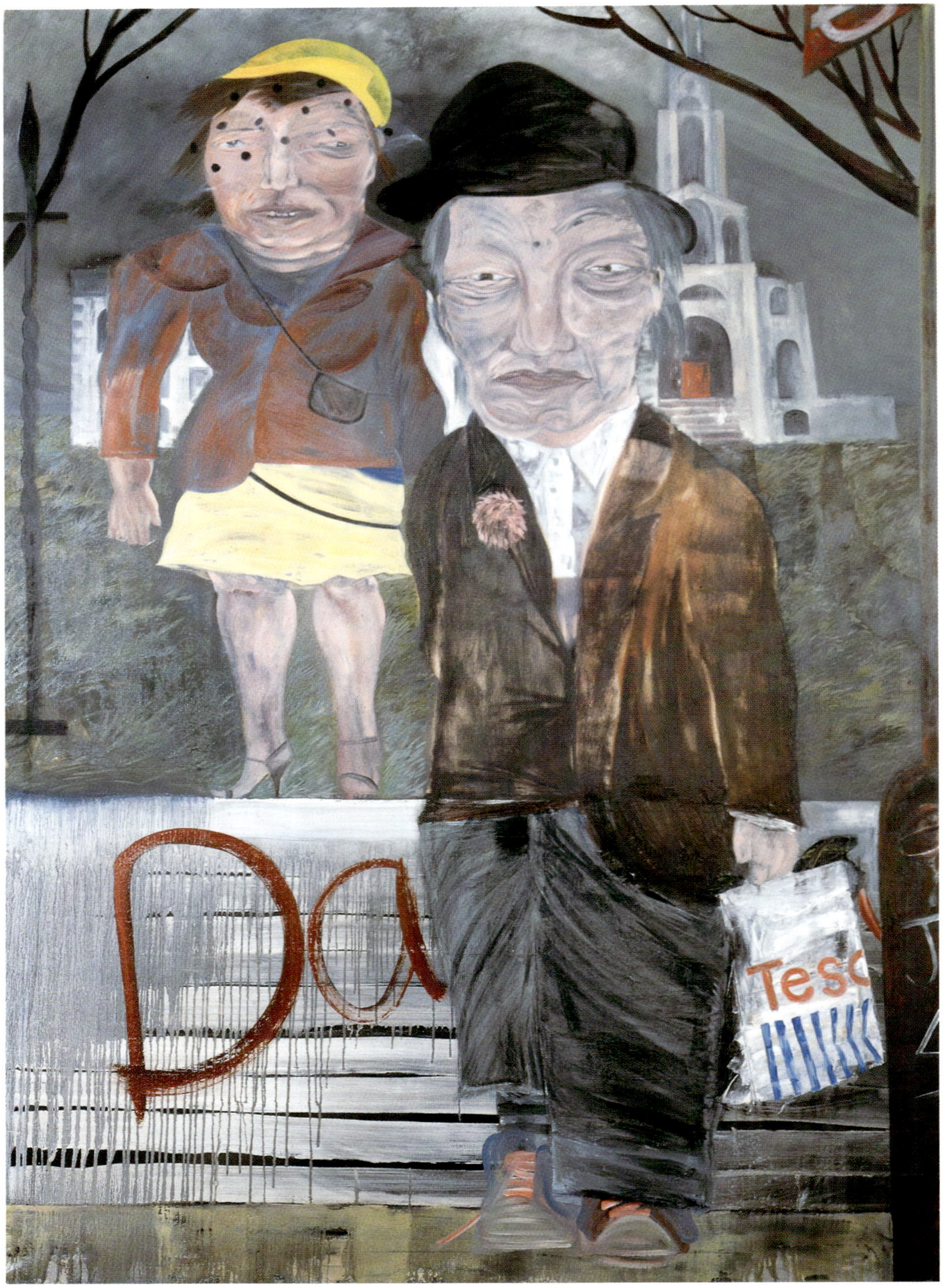

Hawksmoor and Tesco, 1988, oil on canvas, 198 x 140 cm, Private collection

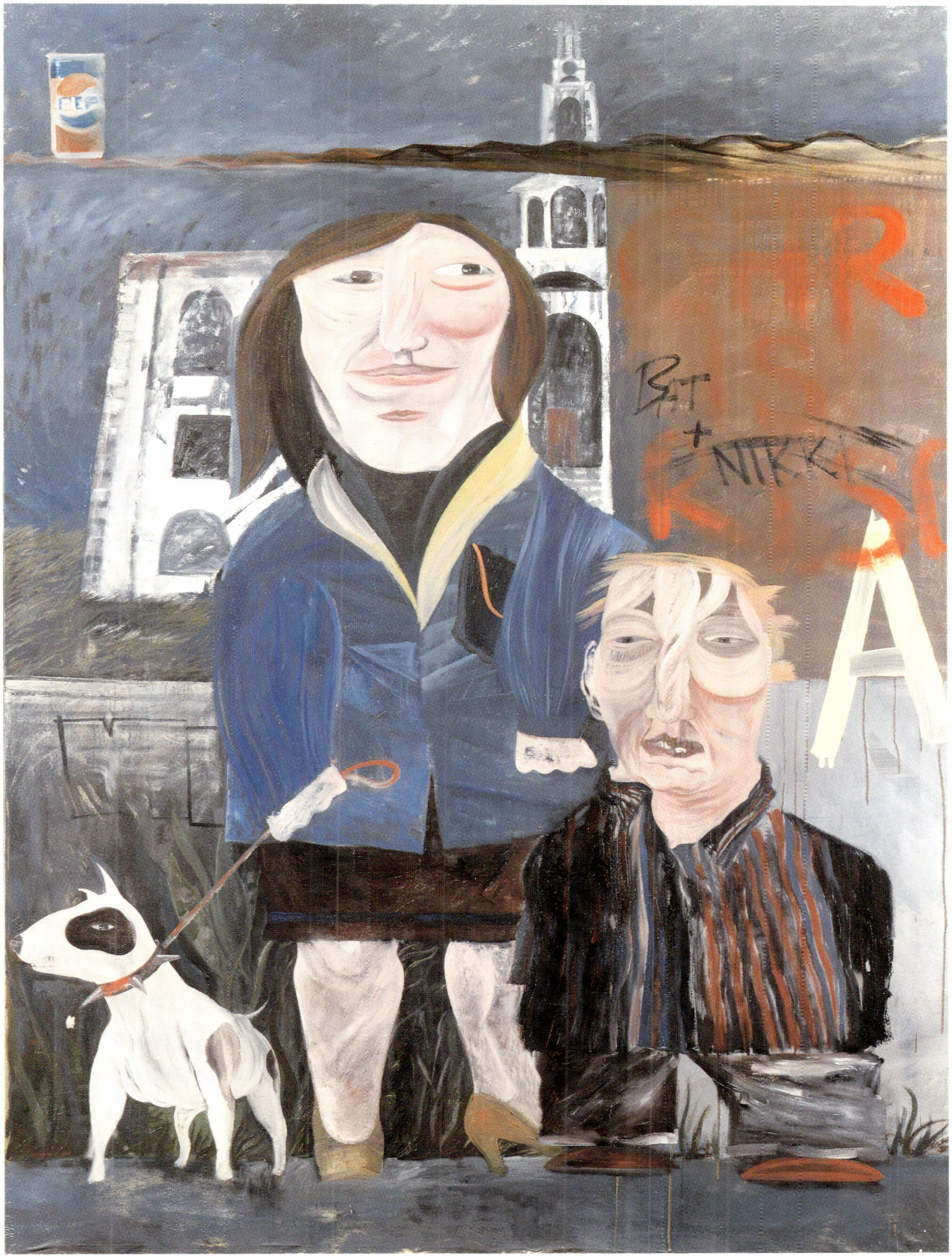

Hawksmoor and Pepsi, 1988, oil on canvas, 208 x 152 cm, Private collection

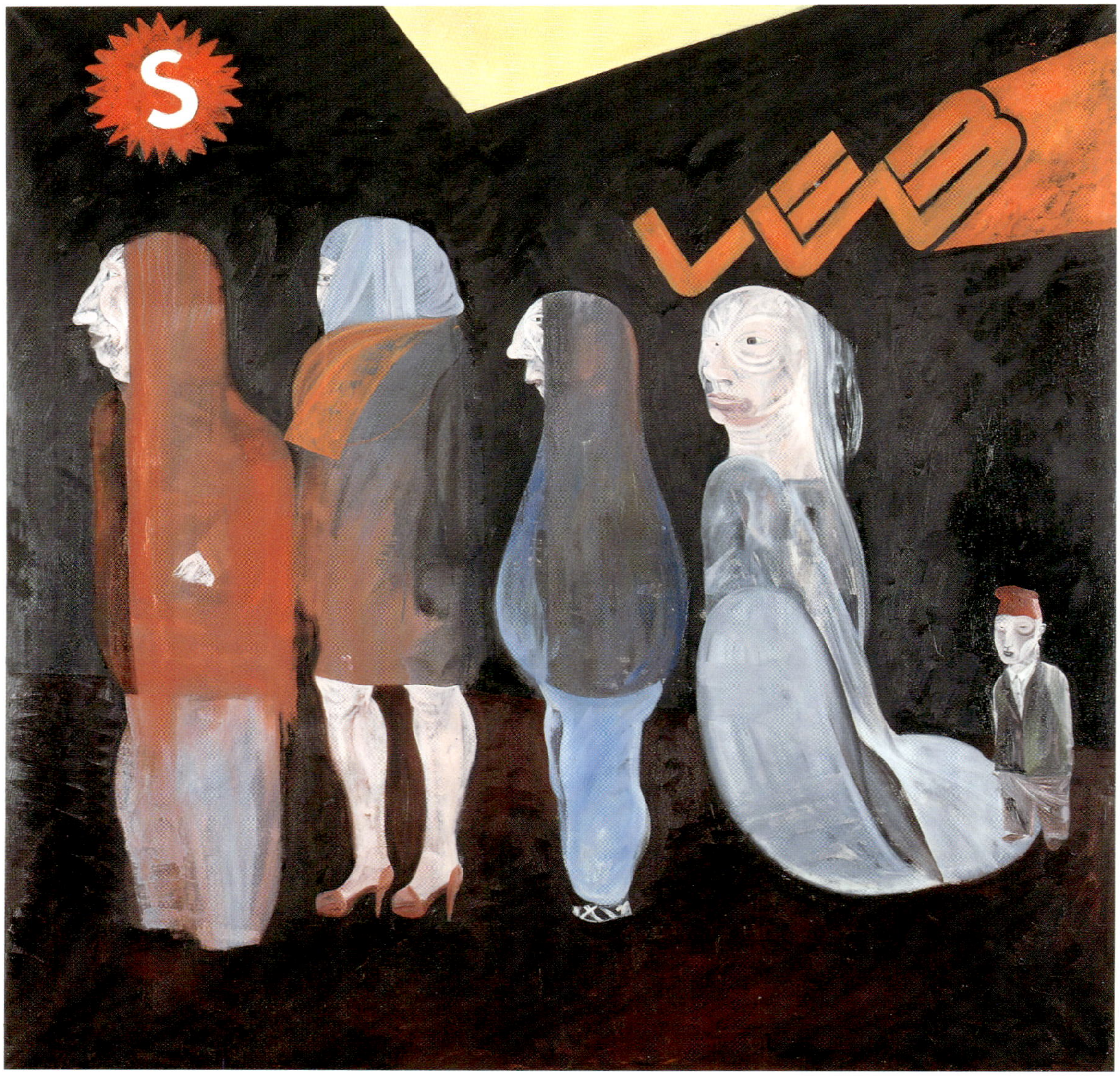

L.E.B, 1989, oil on canvas, 153 x 153 cm

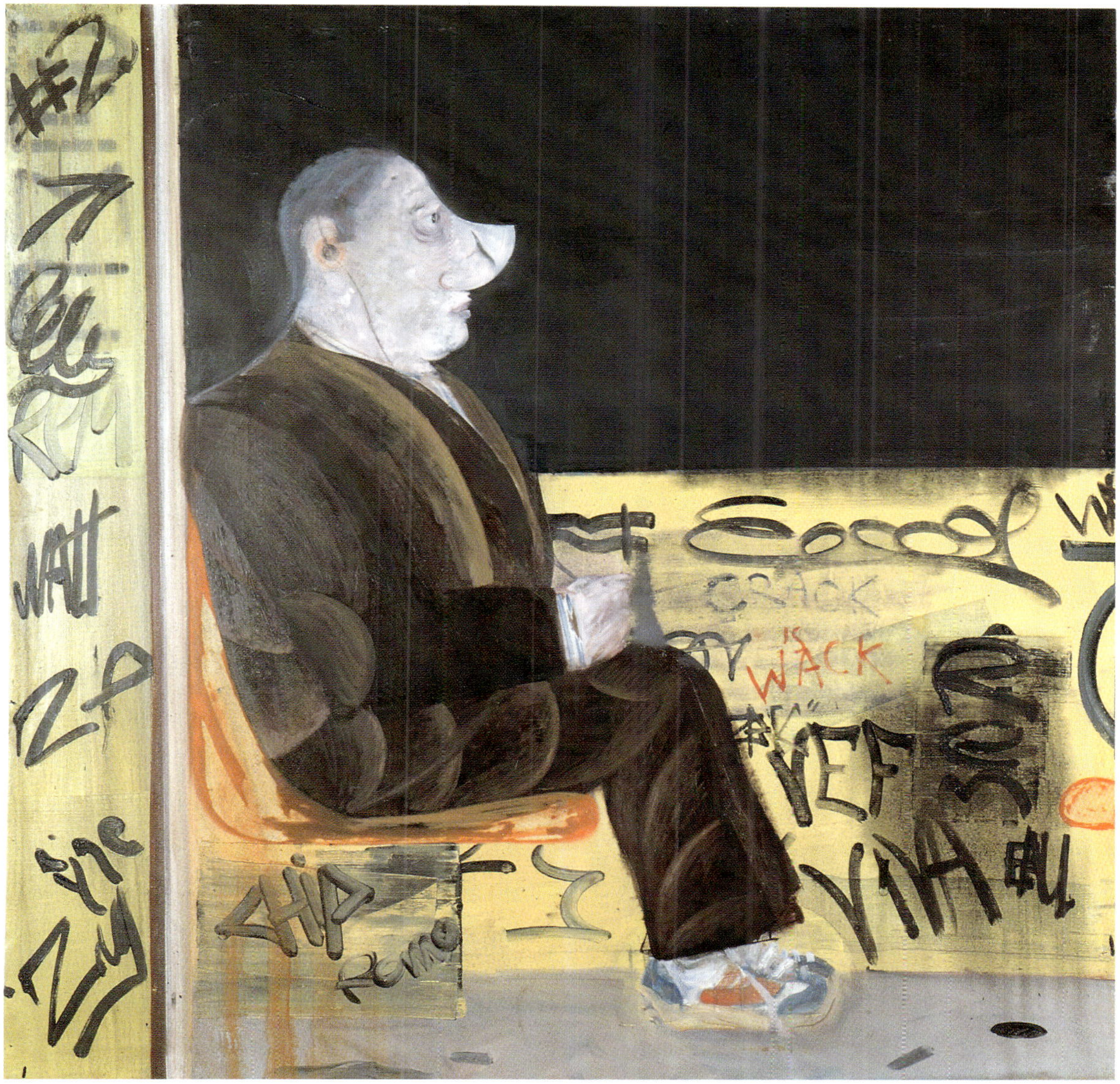

New York Subway, 1988, oil on canvas, 153 x 153 cm, Private collection

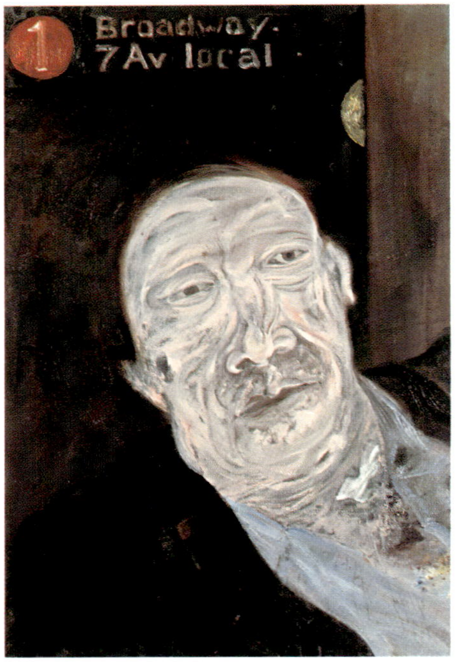

Broadway and 7th Avenue Local, 1990
oil on canvas, 101 x 71 cm, Private collection

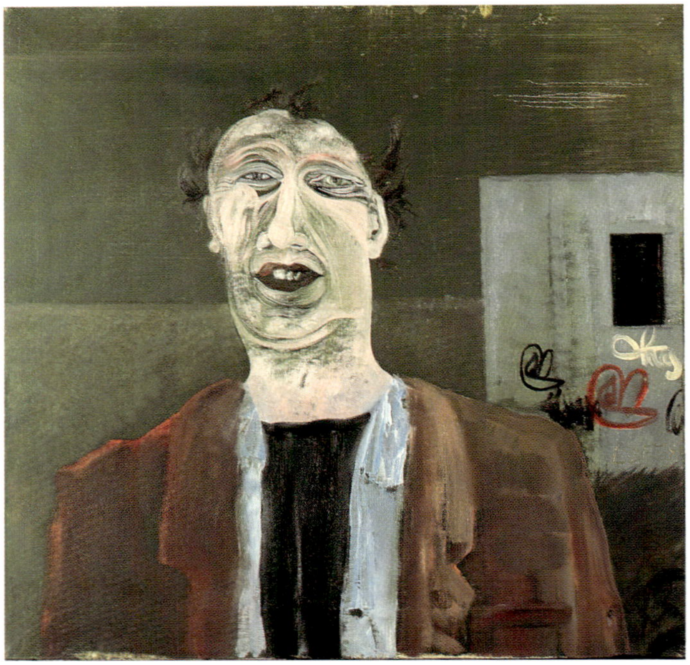

Limehouse Basin, 1990
oil on canvas, 90 x 90 cm, Private collection

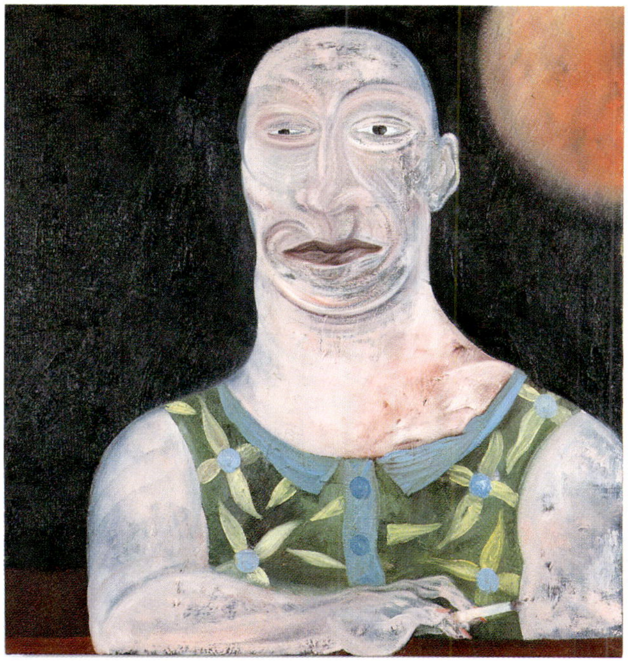

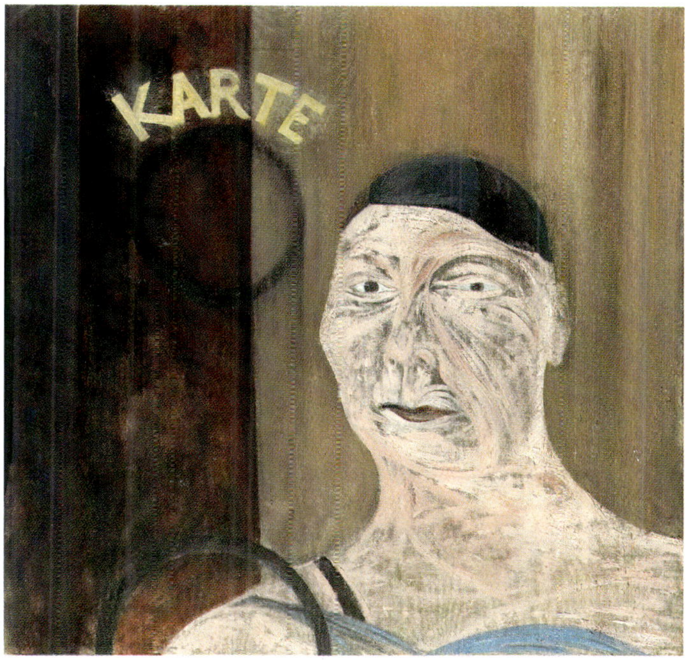

Nitelite, 1989
oil on canvas, 86 x 78 cm

Booth, 1991
oil or canvas, 95 x 95 cm

grooves chiselled into the character's features betray an inescapable phrenology that index-links his disfigurement to his crimes, whether committed or latent.

If McFadyen's faces, for all their highly evolved individualism – and each one is passionately unique – are still somehow generic, this may have something to do with the artist's working method. 'All the people from this time are a mixture of people I have seen, and me', he says. 'Subjects would be stalked, secretly photographed sometimes and strongly remembered. In the studio, when this recipe faltered, there would be recourse to a mirror.' The cool, unsentimental scrutiny the artist brings to his own features licenses strangeness: poky, slitted eyes, an intensity at the bridge of the nose, contour lines flowing into and out of this pivot point, contracting nostrils, pursed lips. Once we know about this self-referential strategy, the ethical balance of his world view shifts. What at first might appear a cocktail of mannerism and misanthropy turns out, on the contrary, to be a hybrid humanism. His people look like this because they are made in his image. There must be a liberating kind of selflessness in populating one's imaginary world with mutations of oneself. The flayed quality need not be read literally: McFadyen people haven't all just been to lunch with Hannibal Lecter. They live happily enough with their disfigurements; indeed, if anything, these disfigurements are thrown back at us, the beholders, made guilty by our presuming to know characters from faces.

In McFadyen's treatment of women, especially prostitutes, strippers and pub dancers sexualised *ad absurdum*, the phrenology of the face is visited on the whole body. A McFadyen stripper must live with the irony that she arrives in the world ready stripped, as it were, in the sinewy tautness of her features, the brushed-in muscularity of her flesh. In *Cabaret*, 1990, the whole of the dancer's figure is taut and contorted, as if she were a rag that had been twisted dry. The dryness of her flesh, contrasted with the glistening sensuality of the background, adds to the oddness and contradiction of this image. Convexes and concaves pushed up against the picture surface twist her out of shape, yet in the erotics of this painterly performance (this cabaret) she comes out compellingly shapely – look at that Picassoesque shoulder, those buttocks expanding within our vision. Appropriately for a work made after McFadyen's time in Berlin, *Cabaret* recalls Otto Dix and a scene from Isherwood's *Goodbye to Berlin*. At the same time, perhaps, it brings to mind the Swiss Romantic painter Henry Fuseli in the mysterious diaphanousness

Text continues on page 38

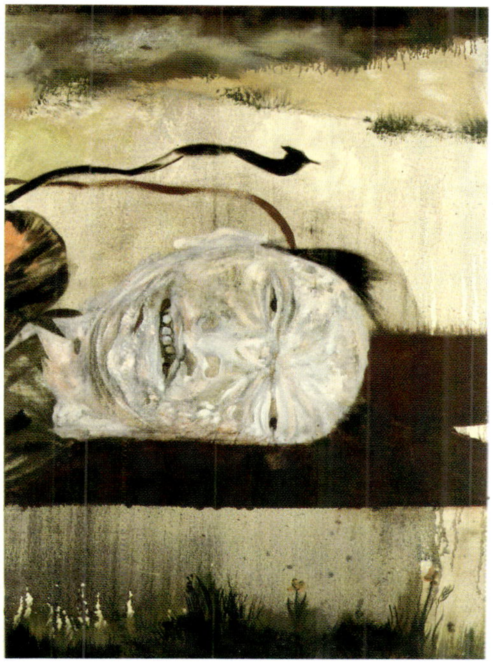

Dead head, 1995, oil on canvas, 86 x 60 cm, Private collection

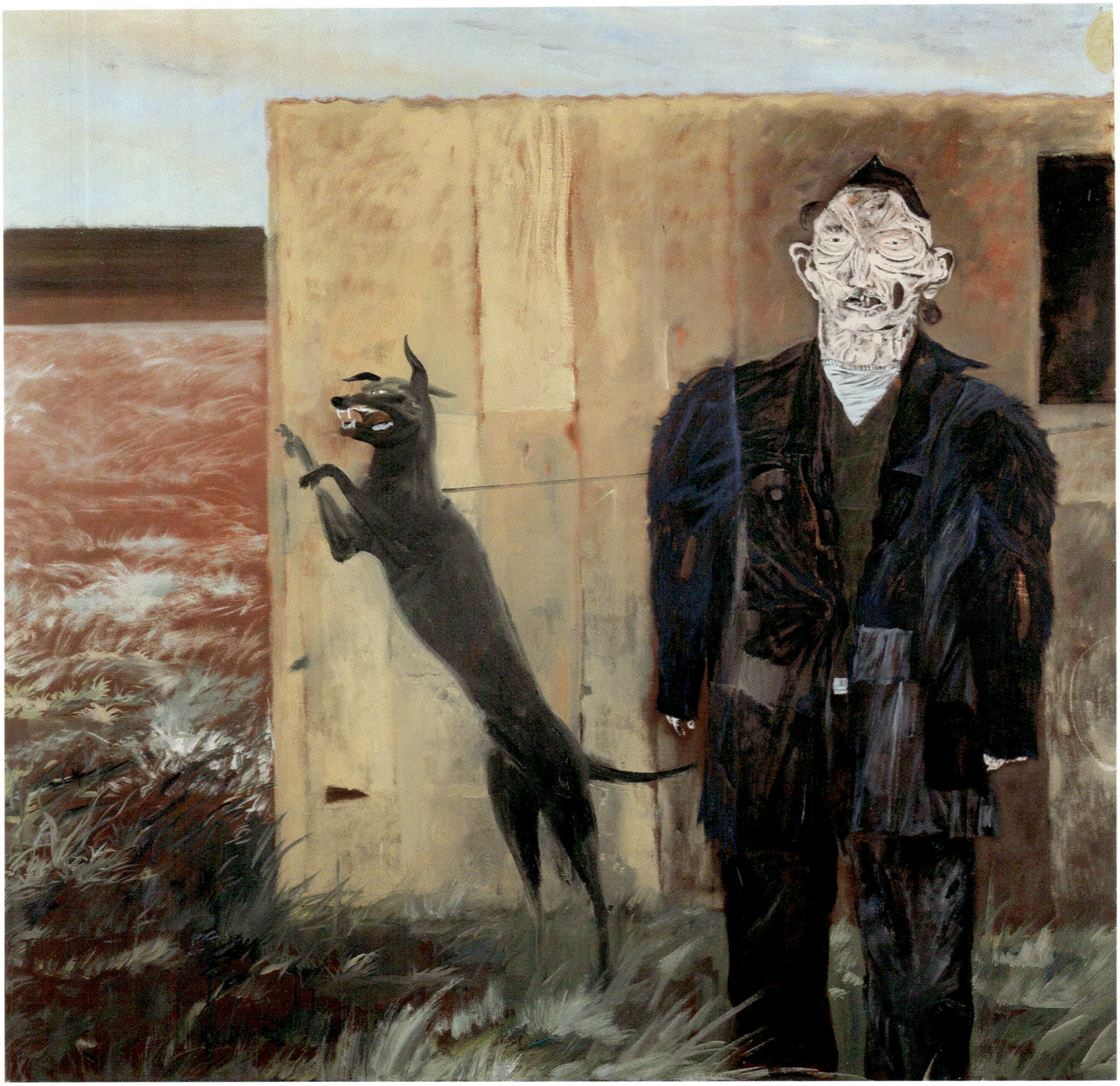

Shelter, 1990, oil on canvas, 168 x 168 cm

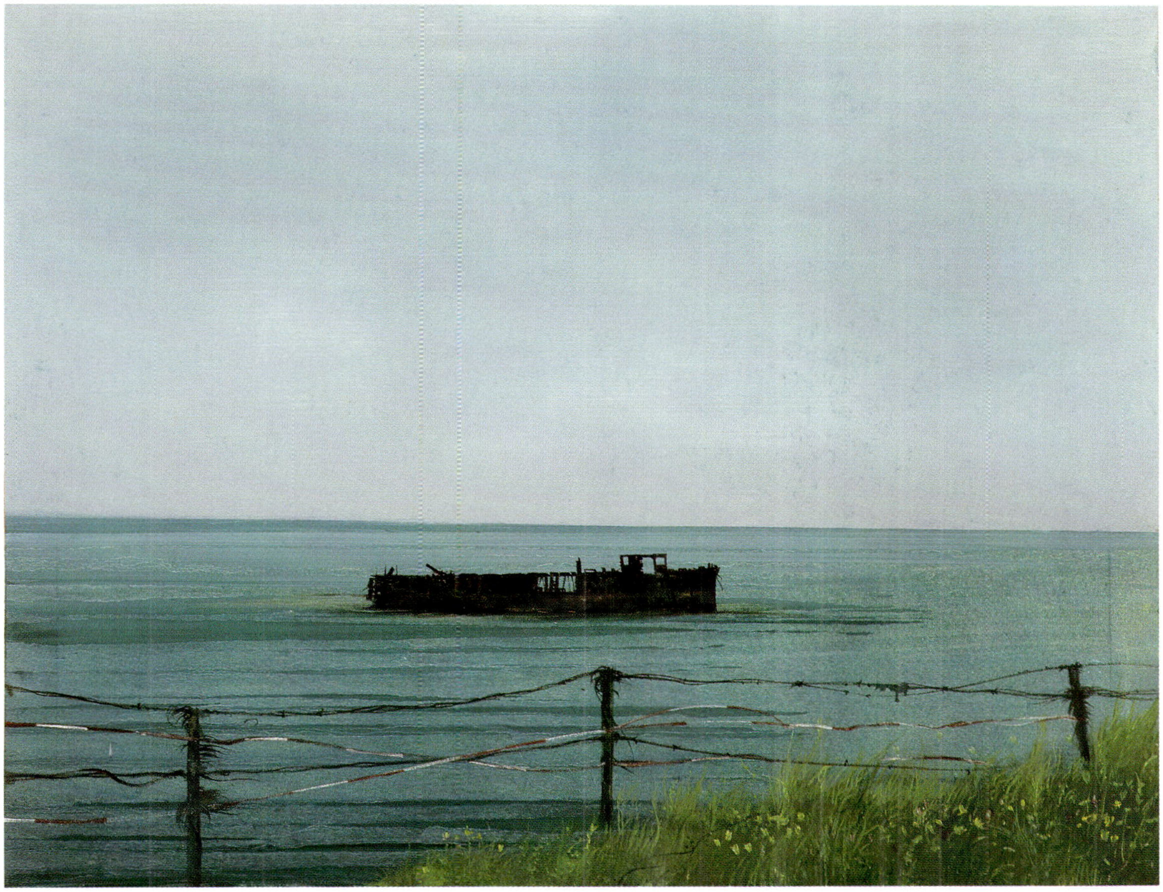

Inganess Bay I, 1999, oil on canvas, 122 x 152 cm

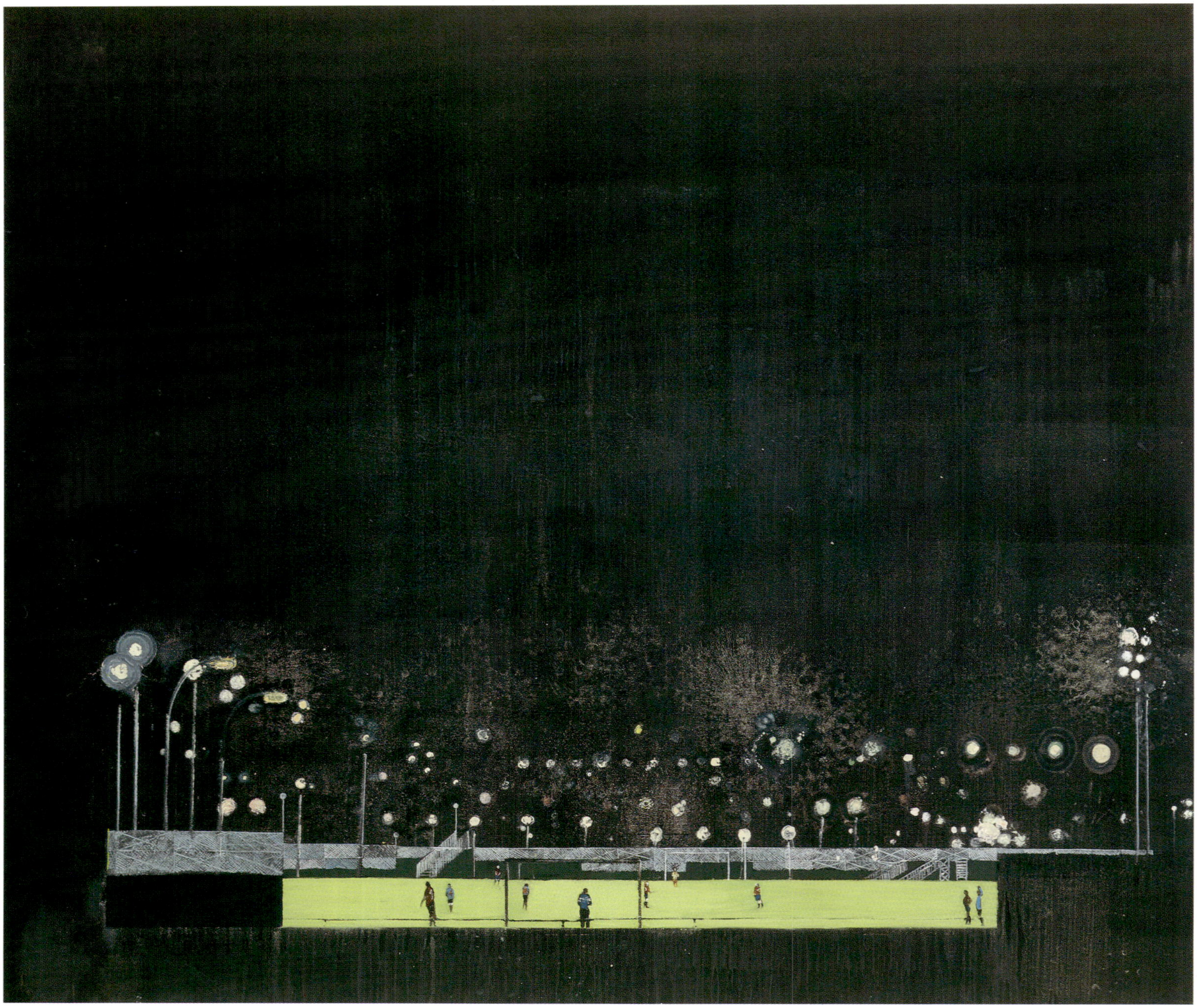

Stadium, 1997, oil on canvas, 178 x 203 cm

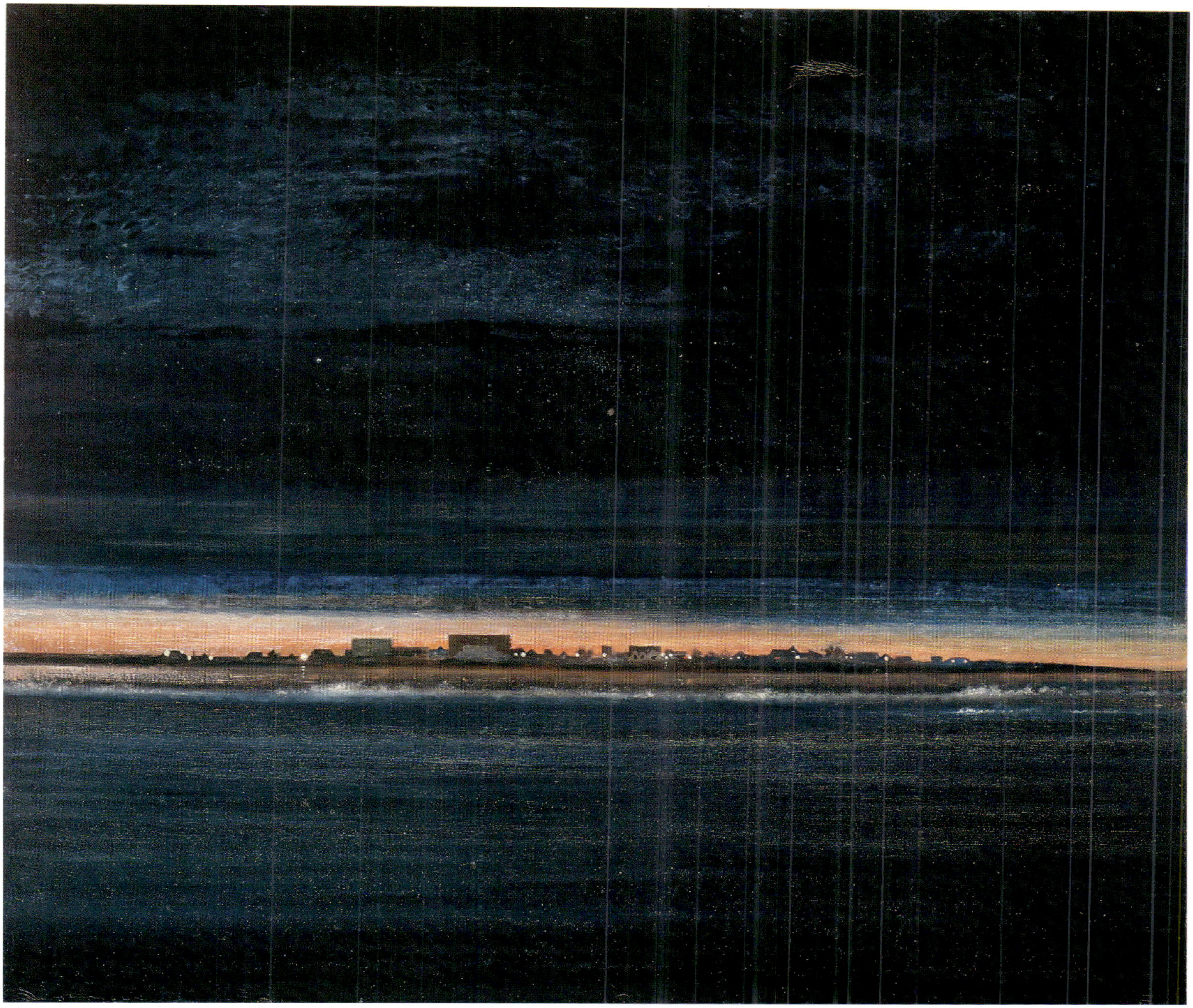

Carnoustie from the sea, 1998, oil on canvas, 178 x 203 cm

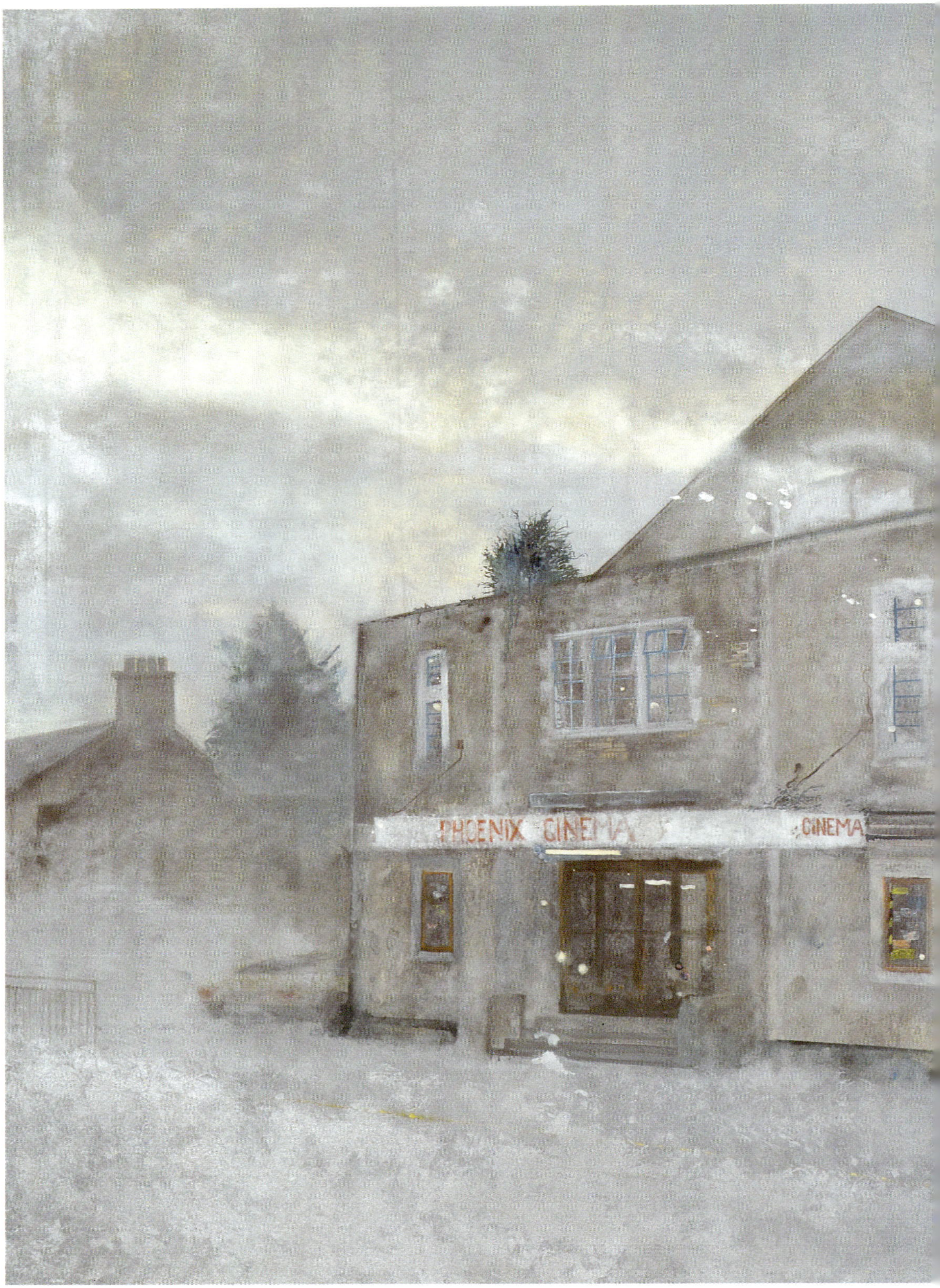

Phoenix, 1999, oil on canvas, 210 x 300 cm

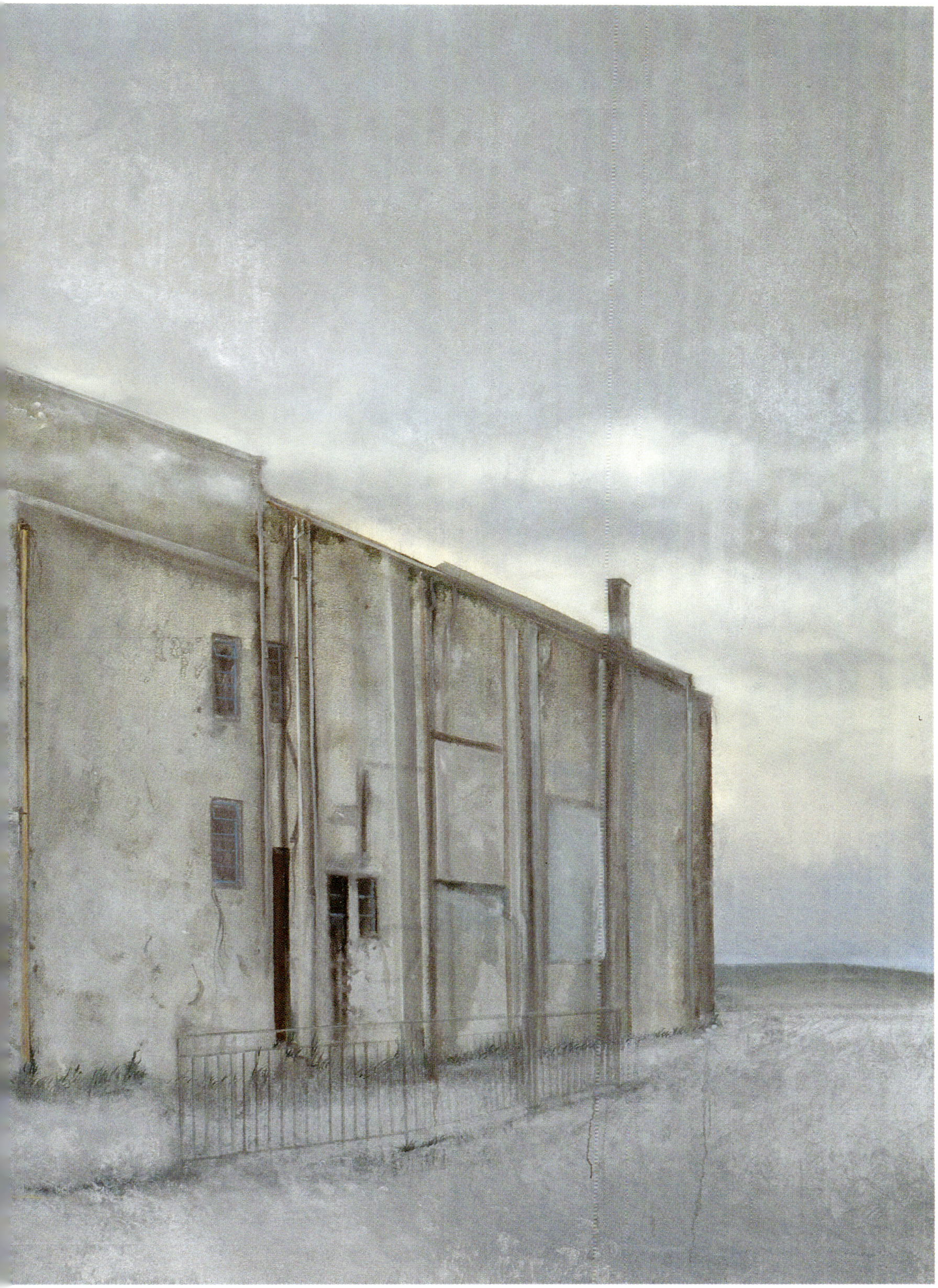

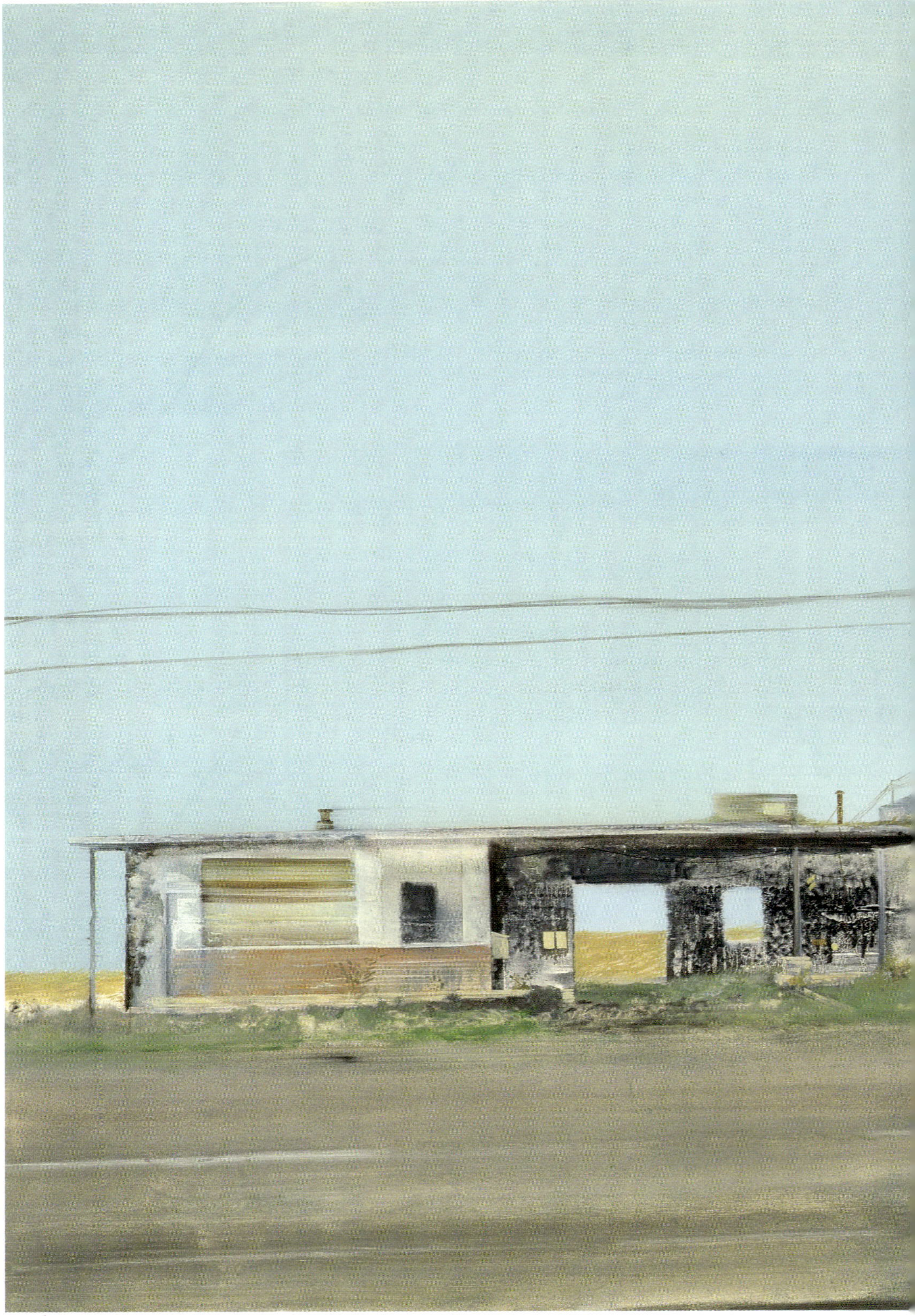

Somewhere in America, 2000, oil on canvas, 178 x 254 cm

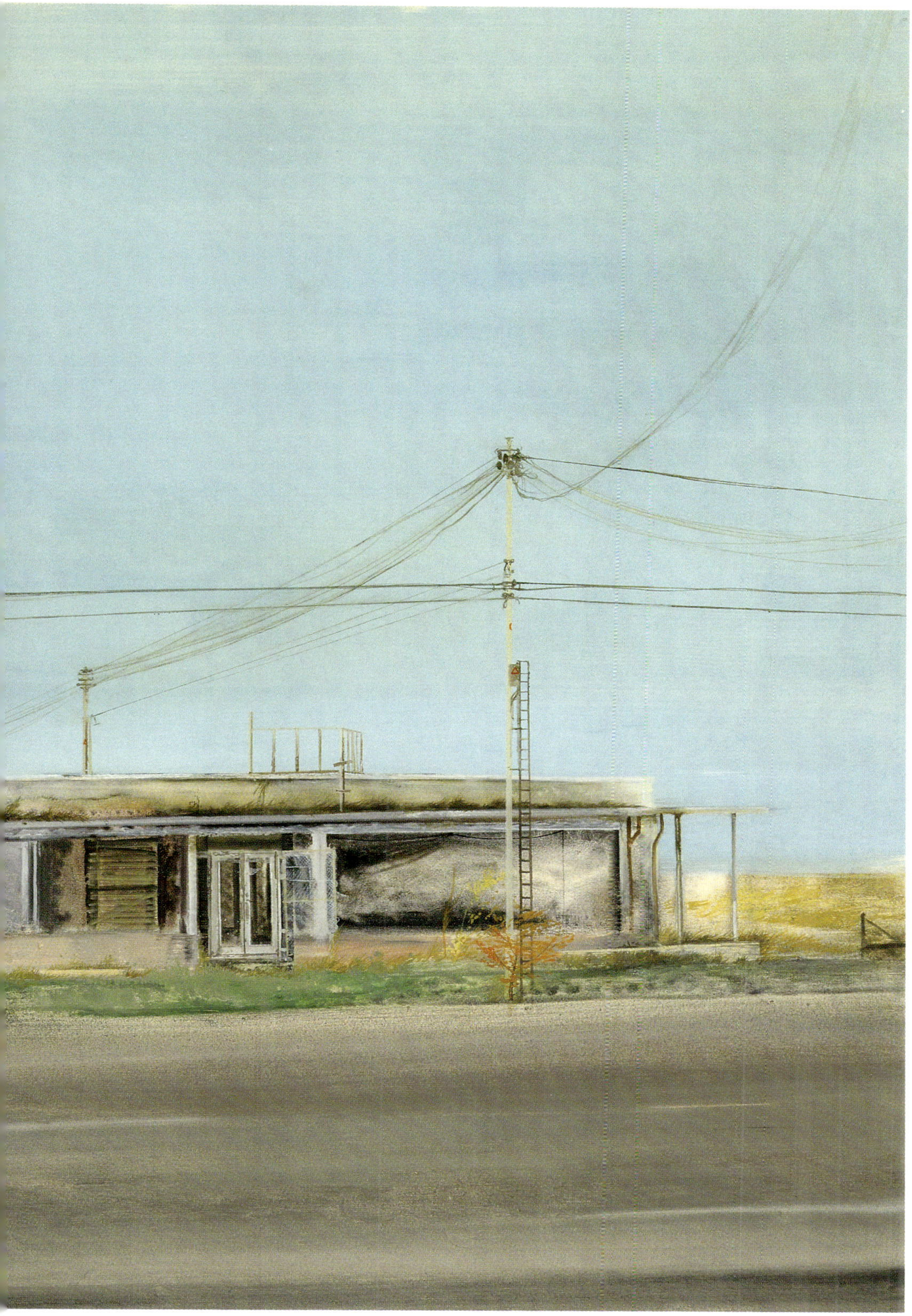

OVERLEAF
Turners Road, 2000
oil on canvas, 173 x 335 cm

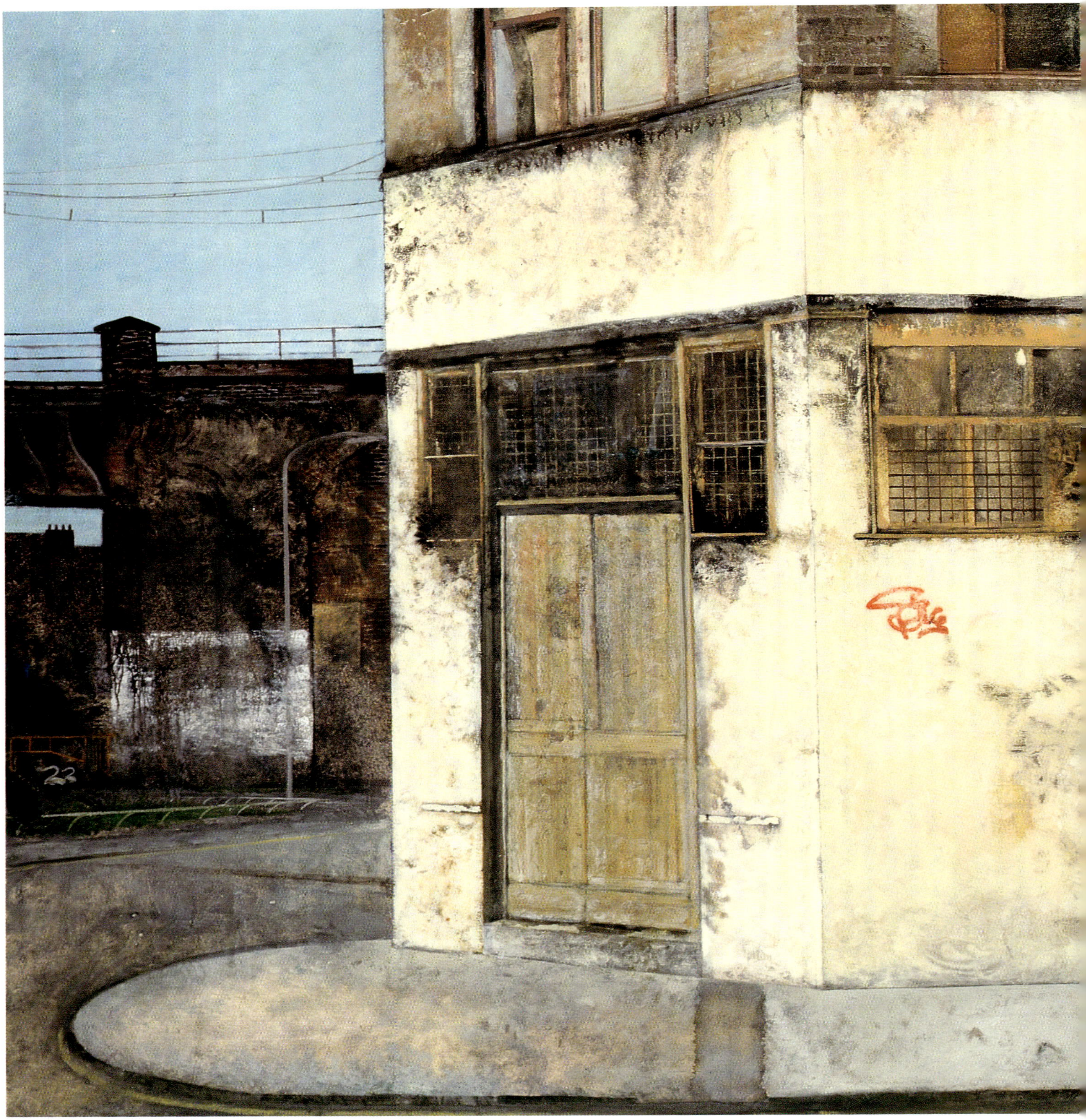

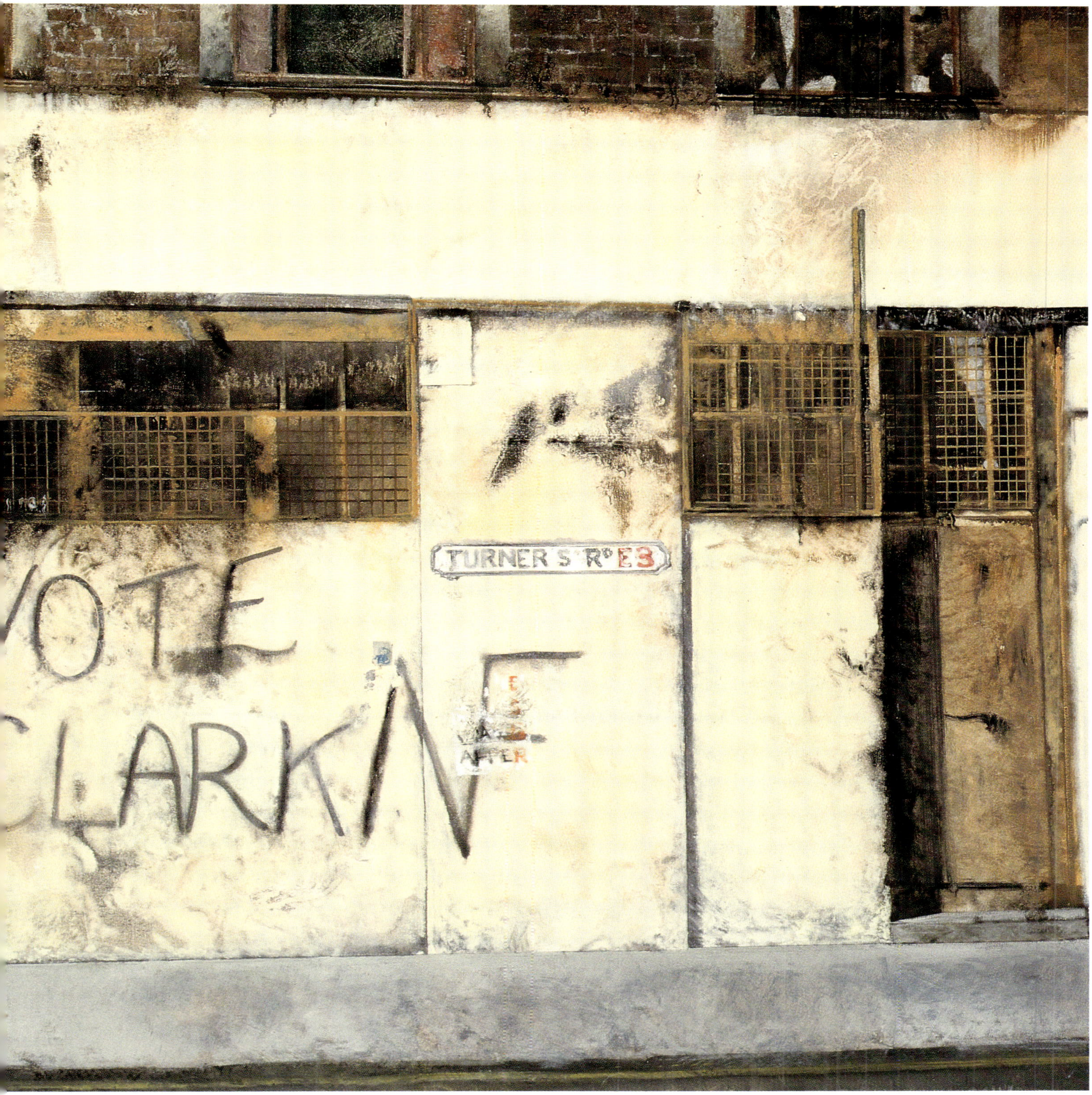
TURNER ST RD E3
VOTE
CLARKIN

Lewis Biggs

Humphrey Ocean

Howard Jacobson

Bob and Roberta Smith

Hugo Williams

Tom Lubbock

Ian Dury

Mary Rose Beaumont

Duncan Macmillan

Jeffery Camp

Will Self

Lewis Biggs

McFadyen in conversation refers constantly to TV, film, magazines and newspapers. His work from 1977 to 1982 borrowed their ready-made imagery freely. He describes this process as 'making an irony' by 'pimping' images from the 'media' into paintings. His phrase suggests the pleasure he derives from illicit dealing in the desirable goods sometimes considered taboo on the art market. But, more importantly, it was idioms as much as images that he borrowed from these other media. An idiom is the turn of phrase which carries the weight of meaning in a sentence, and may even contradict the literal sense of the words [...].

Burt was so handsome that all girls between the ages of sixteen and sixty promptly bumped into lamp-posts at the very sight of him (1979) has its origins in a feature about Hollywood in the *Mirror*. The idiom is not from film but from the strip cartoon – the placing of the two parts of the action in close proximity, the visualisation of a collision, the Desperate Dan jaw of the uproariously laughing Burt. The dynamism of the subject is maximised by making the protagonists face in opposite directions. At the same time the painting owes its realisation, and perhaps much of its motivation, to the incorporation of fine art references: the encaustic paint and star pattern from Jasper Johns' 'flag' paintings, the sketchy graphic handling from Hockney. The joke is reproduced on several levels, but its criticism of the sexism inherent in the film industry is no less present or effective for its lightness of touch.

Extract from the essay 'Realism in Art, or a Slap in the Face with a Wet Kipper' from the catalogue for McFadyen's solo touring exhibition *Jock McFadyen: Paintings*, 1986

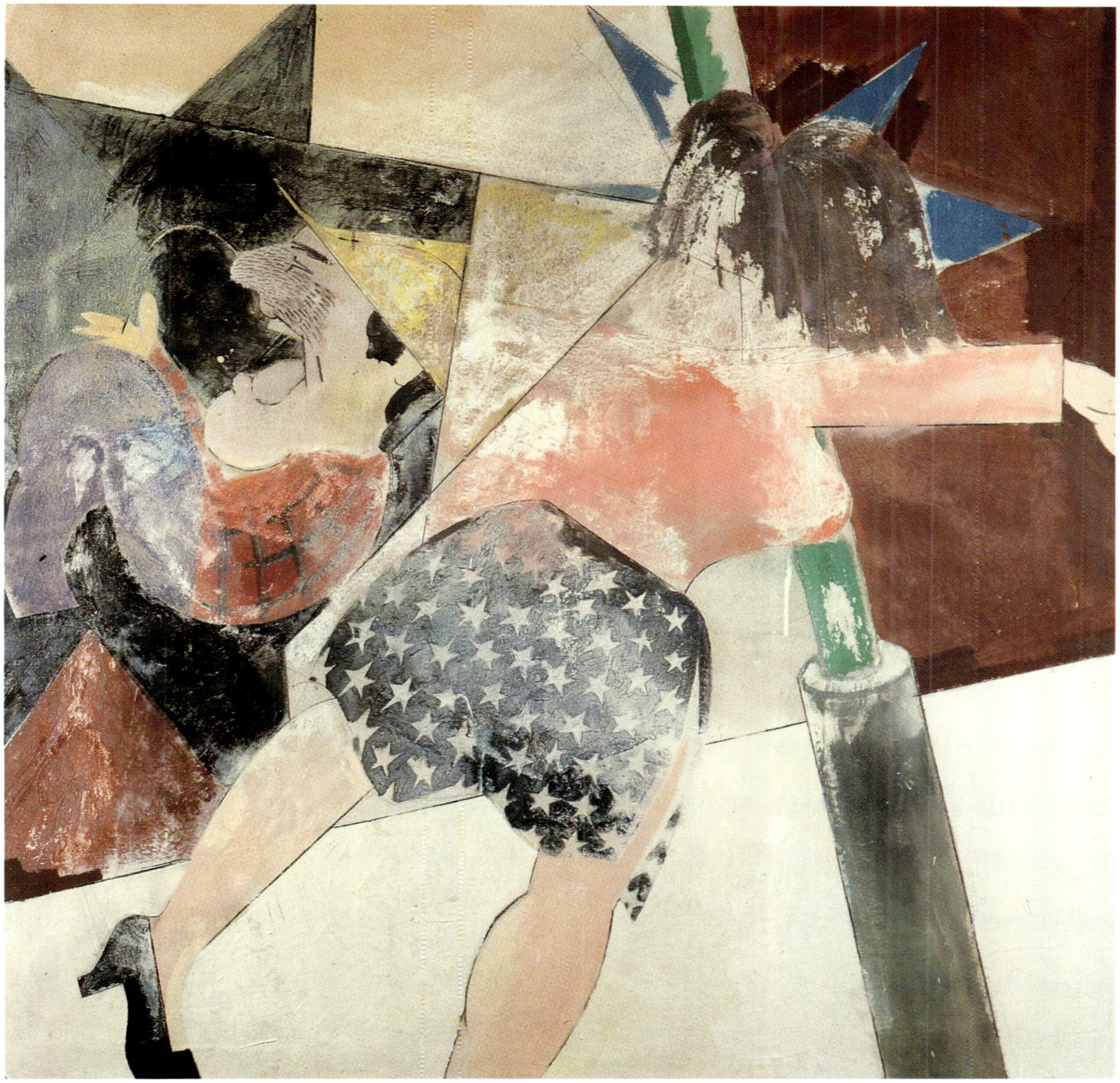

Burt was so handsome that all girls between the ages of sixteen and sixty promptly bumped into lamp-posts at the very sight of him, 1979
oil on canvas, 152 x 152 cm, Private collection

Humphrey Ocean

When Kenneth MacMillan was staging his ballet *The Judas Tree* at Covent Garden, he said that for the set he wanted urban dereliction. Get Jock McFadyen, he said, which was right because there the pictures are set, but for McFadyen dereliction is just one element in a landscape of extremes. You made this, the paintings say, you must deal with it. And the people who are doing so, the stripper, the couple fucking on tussocky waste, the man sitting under a forty watt glare in the minicab office are in no way tragic, pathetic or defeated. Life goes on, pretty much like everybody's. The paintings, although containing moments that are common and recognisable, are themselves entirely singular. Jock McFadyen, surprisingly, is a Scotsman but he has lived half of his life in London and a good proportion of that in eastern postcodes. His viewpoint is different (I maintain) to a Londoner's. There is no 'work is the curse of the drinking classes' morality here, no mawkish sentimentality. When McFadyen includes graffiti, it is not an accessory, the whole painting is as urgent and deft as if he himself were in imminent danger of arrest for criminal damage. His painting rides over our best-laid preconceptions. It can be tender. It suggests that the urine against a wall might have a reassuringly human smell, placidly accepts that concrete is part of planning a town and there, sooner or later, you will uncover all the vicissitudes and glorious skulduggeries the mind and flesh are heir to. Even his unpopulated views of tube stations or London cinemas and bingo halls, deadpan as they are, are fraught with menace. You made this, the Glaswegian says, this is your corner that is forever England. You deal with it.

Humphrey Ocean, January 1997

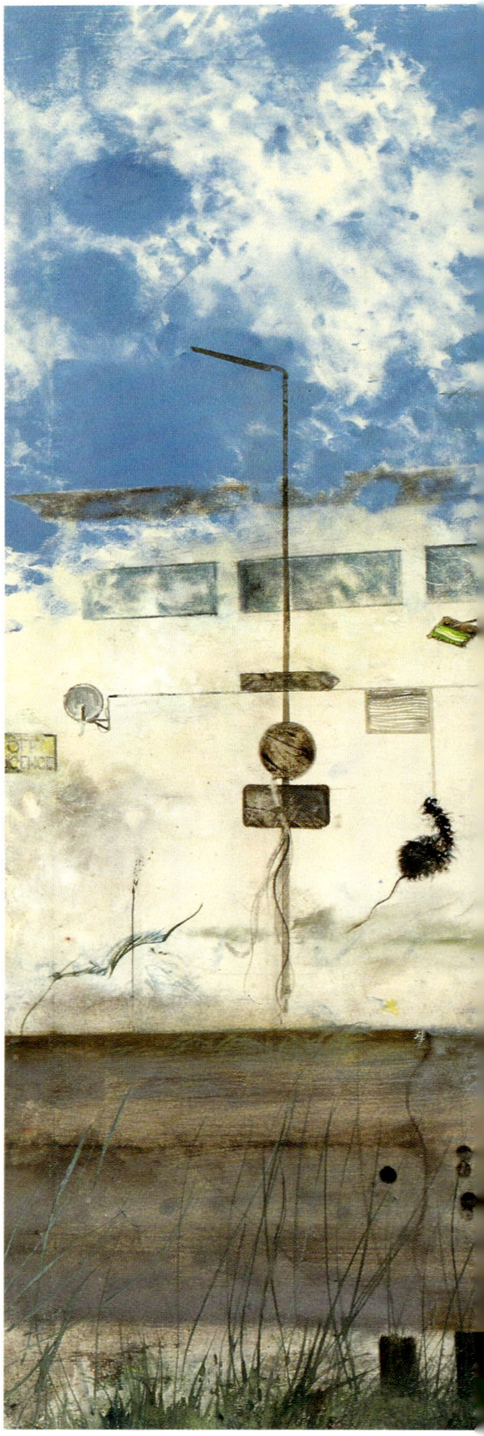

A13, 2000, oil on canvas, 168 x 254 cm

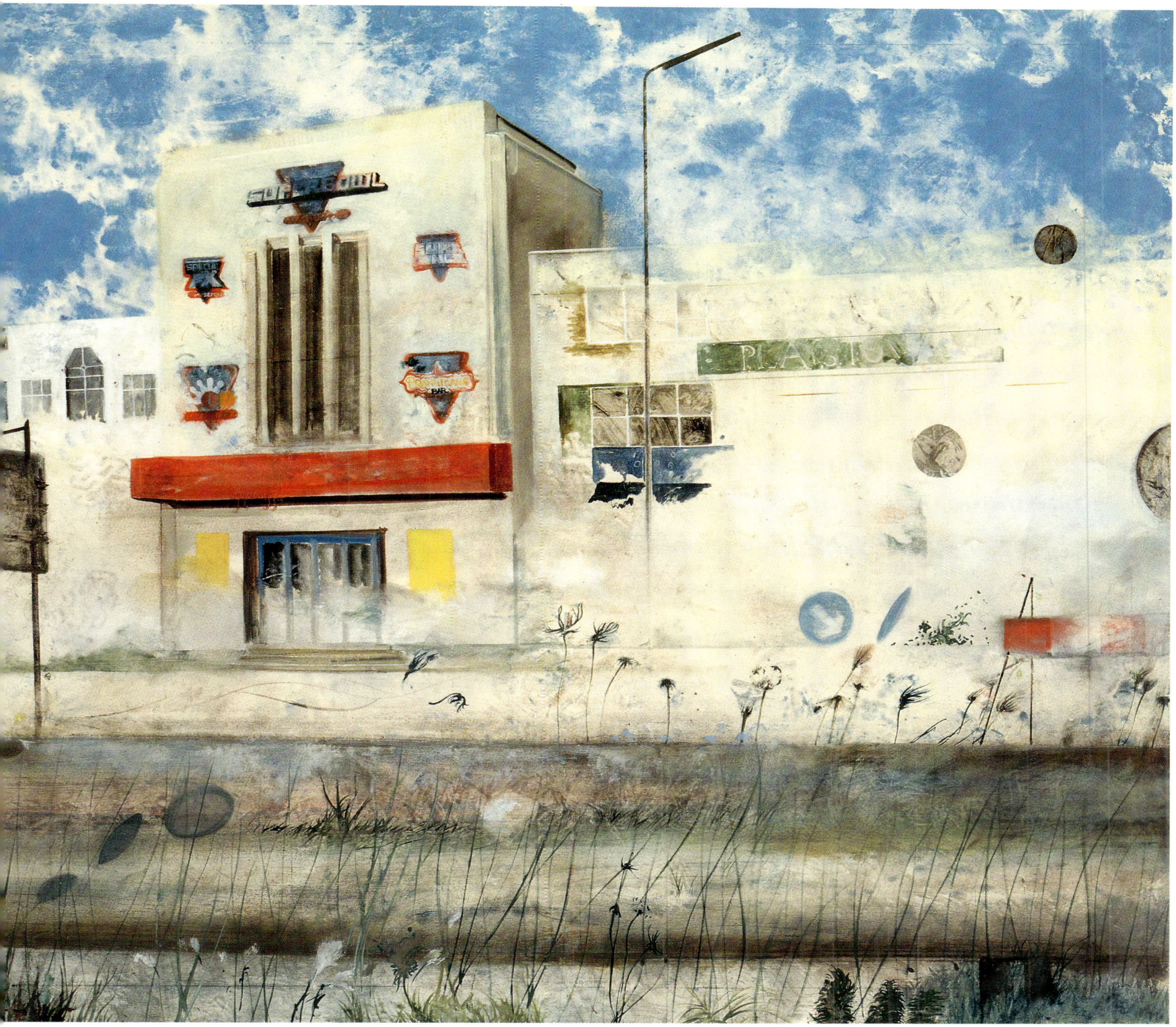
PLASTICA

Howard Jacobson

Try commiserating with any of Jock's urban castaways, try pity on them or charity or socialism, and you soon discover how closed they are to compassion. Not hostile to it, simply impervious. Their eyes do not meet your eyes. Their bodies do not have the flexuousness required for entreaty or gratitude or even, come to that, for curiosity. Quite frankly they are not interested in you, or in what you think, at all.

Close up, there is something a bit fishy about McFadyen's street-loungers and nightlifers, his resolutely unsensual strippers, his wide-thighed women positioned, as though they have grown there like barnacles, on the bonnets of beaten-up cars. They look amphibious, capable of surviving in some other element, all expectation of pleasure on dry land washed away by those tides whose traces one can still read in the whorls around their eyes. Closer up yet, you realise that they are fashioned to withstand wind as well as water, fire as well as air. The thick impasted pink of their flesh is tougher than the meat most of us think we are made of; it looks uncomfortable to wear, but protective, edificial, like plaster or stucco – a skin the colour and texture of gypsum. Awaiting finish, but just as likely to repel paint as pity.

As for the oceans from which they once emerged, or, as in the case of the most recent sculptures, the bogs and marshes out of which they seem still to be climbing, there is no mistaking their geography. It's cold where the creatures have been, however skimpy their clothes. It's a Dutch dejection they brace themselves against, a Breughel-blindness that hollows the sockets of their sight. It helps, I think, when pondering the extraordinary resilience of life as Jock McFadyen paints and sculpts it, to recall that there is such a thing as a Northern imagination, an Arctic as opposed to a Mediterranean cast of mind, and that it finds more to admire in harshness than in ease, more that is native to it in obduracy than in luxury.

Extract from the catalogue foreword for McFadyen's solo exhibition *Canal* at the William Jackson Gallery, London, 1991

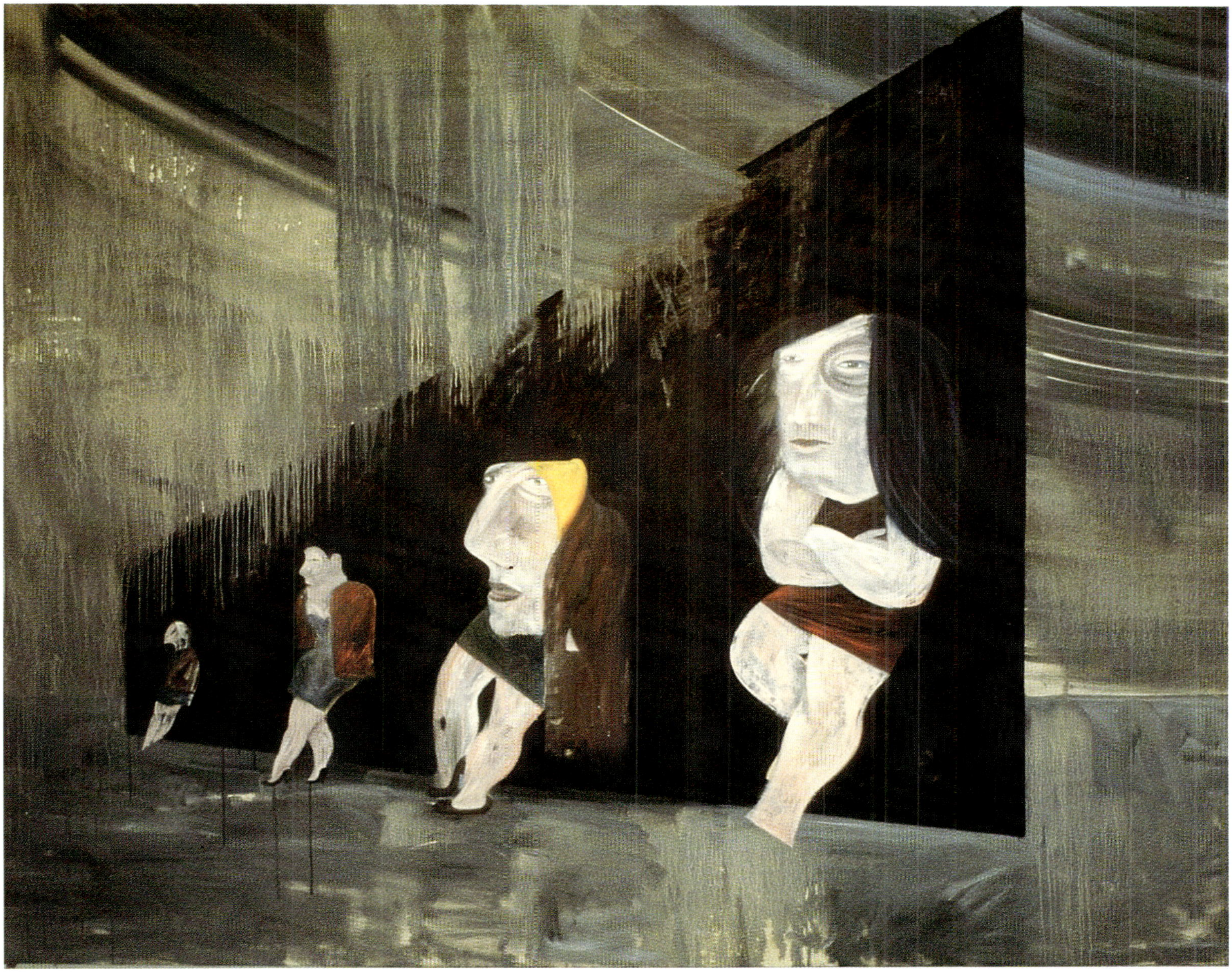

Rainy day women, 1985, oil on canvas, 213 x 244 cm, The Hit Factory

BOB AND ROBERTA SMITH'S STUDIO 1983
IN WALKS VISITIN LECTURER JOCK MC FADYEN

BOB.
HELO JOCK
JOCK.
DO YOU LIKE HOSPITAL FOOOD? WHO DO YOU FINK YOU ARE? FUKIN MATTISE OR SOME BODY? WHATS WITH ALL THIS ARTY DRAWING? YER PAINTINGS ALL LOOK HALF FINNISHED .
BOB.
WELL JOCK. I LIKE TO LEAVE SOME OF THAT STUFF. IT SHOWS HOW THE PAINTIN WAS MADE.
JOCK.
OH, FOR GOODNES SAKE. YOU WOODN'T SAY THAT IF YOU WER FIXING THE WING OF YOUR CORTINA. YOU WOOODN'T LEAVE BRUSH STROKES IN THE BODY FILLER AND BITS OF FIBRE GLASS MESH STICKING OUT TO SHOW HOW CLEFER YOU WERE .
BOB.
YOU'RE RITE JOCK. I'LL HAVE TO CHANNEL MY INTEREST IN BLUNDERS AND MISTAKES IN ANOTHER DIREKSHON.
JOCK
TOO RIGHT. PICK A WINDOW YOUR LEAVING!

A SHORT SCUFFLE THEN BRAKES OUT.

In this extract from the Bob and Roberta Smith Diaries
the part of Jock McFadyen is played by Sean Connery.
Bob Smith is played by Michael Caine.

NOW COLOUR IN

Bob and Roberta Smith, 2000

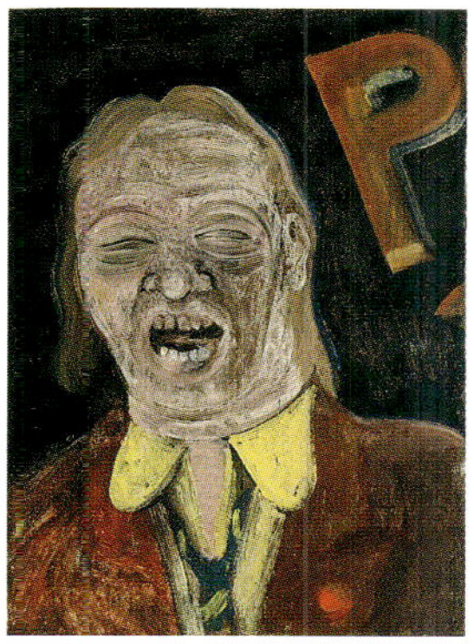

Shouting man, 1995, oil on canvas, 26 x 18 cm, Private collection

Hugo Williams

Jock is so easy-going about the fate of his paintings that he is prepared to let one of them set out on a highly unpredictable journey, the first lap of which will be on the back of my motorbike. He has a bike himself, a Moto Guzzi, which I have difficulty keeping up with, as we leave his house in the East End for his studio in Brick Lane. As a curtain-raiser to his studies of London characters in settings of urban despair and blight, we stop off at the sign saying 'Exotic Dancers' on the corner of the street in Spitalfields where Gilbert and George live.

The Ten Bells, the East End's premier lunchtime strip pub, used to be called The Jack the Ripper, until a feminist campaign enlisted the help of the *Evening Standard* to have the name changed. Despite the correction, the bar still does a brisk trade in Ripper- and stripper-ware (mugs, T-shirts, guide books) and is now packed with sweating lower-order City types, in drip-dry shirts, holding pints. A slim and graceful Asian girl with very long hair passes among them with a glass containing nothing smaller than pound coins, to which we contribute. I notice that in the middle of the room is a pillar surrounded by a few feet of worn carpet.

Dispensing with tease as such, the girl suddenly lets slip her dress and for a second a naked slave is standing at auction among a crowd of shirt-sleeved businessmen. Her music restores us to more acceptable roles, and we are treated to a series of bodily revelations which out-stare even these male gazes. What's fascinating and impressive about it, rather than erotic, is the relaxed expression on her face; she must have a mental knack which enables her to dominate this hell-hole. I wonder how many others present identify with her courage. Behind her, on the wall, is a wooden panel listing the names and brief histories of the six women murdered by Jack the Ripper. In this corner of London where Asian faces outnumber Caucasian, it is the Englishness of the names – Turner, Nicholls, Chapman, Eddowes – which are now exotic. As we leave, we pass a doorway full of neatly ranged oriental slippers; inside, heads bowed down in midday prayer.

Jock's studio is in Brick Lane itself, which might be a back street in Calcutta – sari shops, Indian music, Bengali tea-rooms: an ironical setting for his decadent, post-Empire cityscapes, with their exhausted loners and drop-outs, such as the stare-eyed derelict half-carrying his mother across Hackney Marshes in her sleeping bag. 'They look amphibious', wrote Howard Jacobson of McFadyen's creatures, 'capable of surviving in some other element, all expectation of pleasure on dry land washed away by those tides whose traces one can still read in the whorls around their eyes.' And it is true that attention focuses on the strange eyes of McFadyen's creations, slitty, ancient, tortoise-eyes, much scored-around, as if they were made of the same impacted scum and flotsam they were looking at.

McFadyen is currently working on a series of defunct cinema facias and decaying tube station interiors: 'The Rex', melting into grime and time with ancient hopeful posters peeling off and rusty corrugated iron hoarding; or 'Kennington Station', where 'you've got people going to work in the biggest city in the world and downstairs it's like the Third World.' In this painting, recent graffiti fight with existing graphics and cabling. 'A lot of the graffiti is well done, then someone will come along and put "West Ham are wankers" over a fantastic piece of New York hip-hop. I have to try to do both for the picture, otherwise it falls into an aesthetic thing ... like the problem of how to do slang in writing.'

Extract from the poet's 'Freelance' column in the *Times Literary Supplement*, 1997

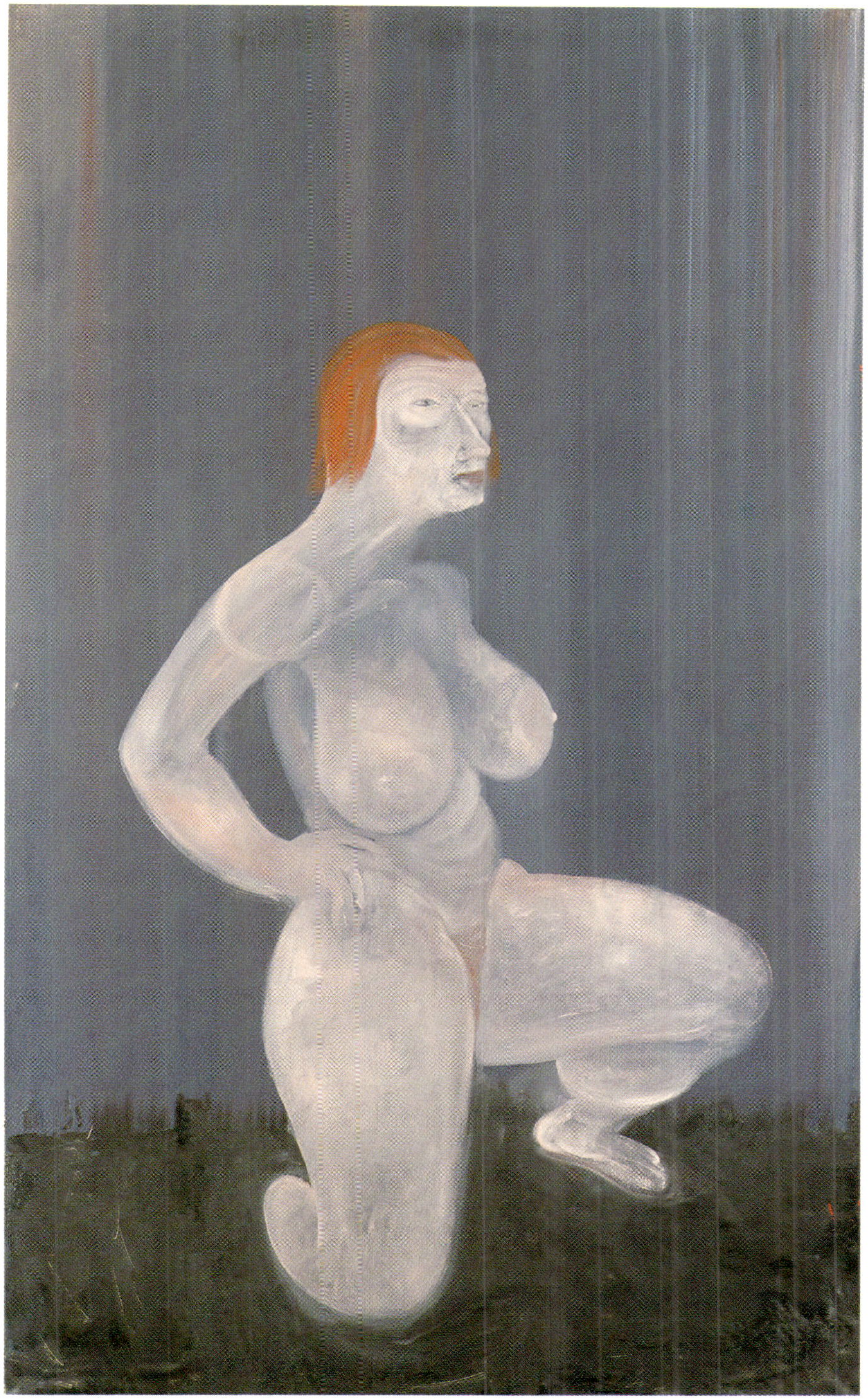

Pub dancer II, 1989, oil on canvas, 193 x 114 cm

Tom Lubbock

There are one or two identifiable landmarks though. East Berlin's Sputnik-style TV tower often stands out. Built by the DDR as assertively the tallest, most ultra-modern building in the city, it now portrays woefully its dated space-age aspirations (it's the kind of superannuation that McFadyen is drawn to). On the other hand, no pictures of the Brandenburg Gate, or of Checkpoint Charlie. He isn't looking for images that 'say it all', or count as 'typical' according to the usual journalistic standards. He works more like a sightseer without a guidebook. It's just what catches his eye.

There is of course The Wall: the wall after it was broken down, the wall with its decorations. This is an inevitable sight for the sightseer, and for McFadyen particularly attractive, being both a wreck, and something covered with all sorts of accretions. In the pictures the wall is viewed from the west side, the side with the graffiti. (Or, more accurately, what we see is the west side of the Western outer wall: along most of its length the wall was two walls, inner and outer, with a wide no-man's land, patrolled and booby-trapped, running between them.) In *Die Mauer*, we see a section chipped through by the wall 'woodpeckers', exposing its metal skeleton, and beyond that a stretch of now vacant no-man's land. In *Christmas in Berlin*, the top of the wall blurs into the background, and the Christmas lights of the east twinkle weakly in the distance.

The wall was a great site for graffiti, and on it graffiti's usual purposes – a mixture of creativity, propaganda, vandalism and territoriality – were magnified. It became a libertarian gesture of a sort: an assault on the wall's oppressive blankness; an actual incursion of the DDR's border and property (since even the outer wall lay technically within Eastern territory); and a piece of magic, a proxy overcoming of the monster. Now it's fallen, only graffitied fragments have any market value.

Faced with this well-established spectacle, a monstrosity and a monument even in ruins, McFadyen offers a plain, full-frontal sight. The wall comes up flat against the picture surface, producing an almost abstract field of marks. With graffiti, it's a general rule that all would-be imitations of it – such as you find in commercial artwork or a stage set – are blatantly unconvincing. You see only an elegant hand aiming uselessly for street credibility.

But here, as far as possible, the graffiti on the wall is authentically transcribed (if slightly rearranged for pictorial purposes). McFadyen deliberately tries to suppress his own habitual gestures and handwriting to observe the character of marks made by dozens of other people. It's a way of not succumbing to the wall's great symbolic weight and opportunities. (Another artist might have been tempted to introduce a few slogans or pictures of his own, an obvious enough way to be meaningful while still looking natural.) McFadyen leaves the graffiti as a random accumulation of conflicting messages, and the wall as a strange, derelict, anomalous lump.

Extract from the catalogue essay for McFadyen's solo exhibition *Fragments from Berlin* at the Imperial War Museum, London, 1991

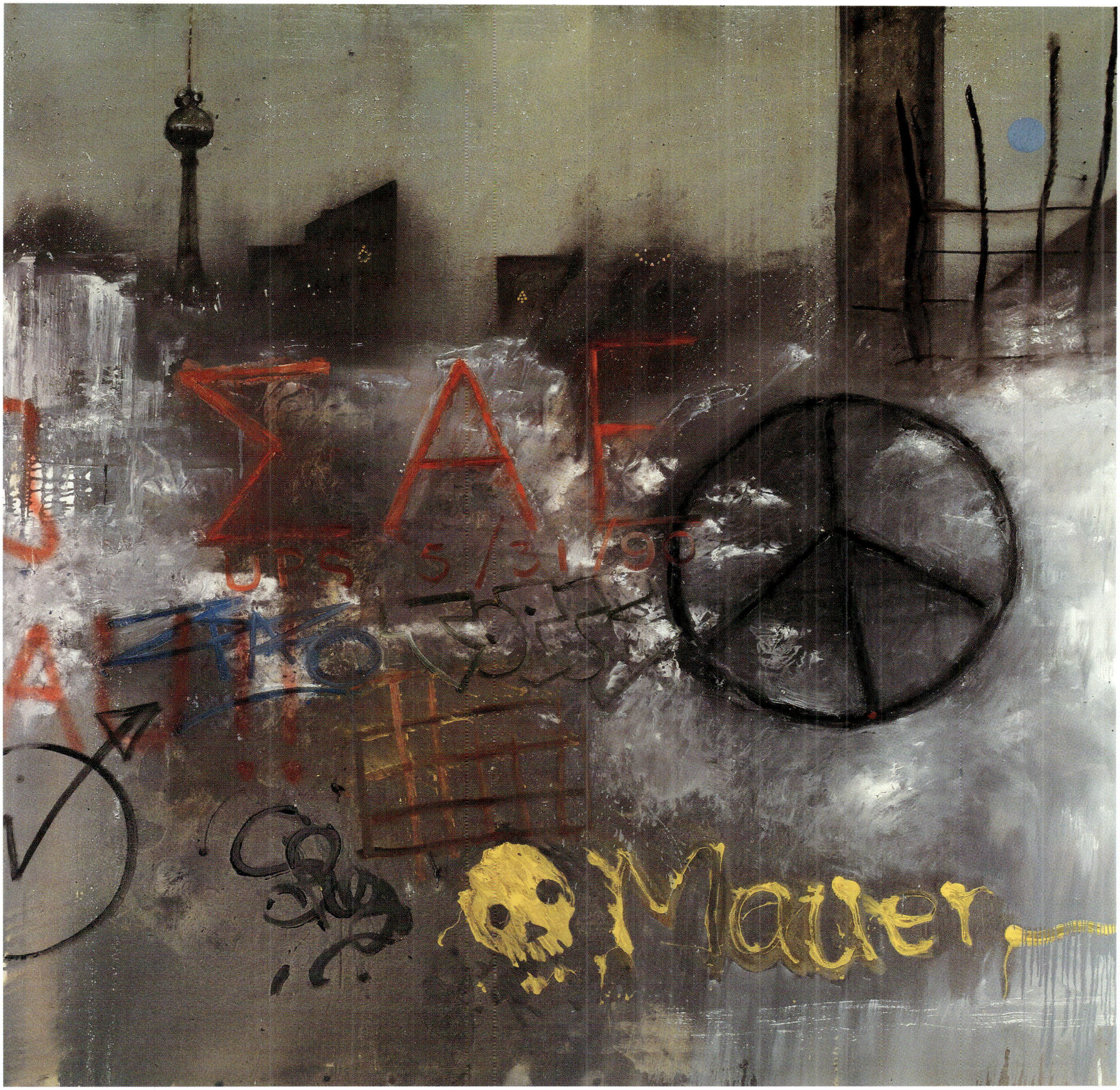

Christmas in Berlin, 1991, oil on canvas, 265 x 265 cm, Imperial War Museum

IAN DURY

Billericay Dickie

Good evening, I'm from Essex, in case you couldn't tell. My given name is Dickie. I come from Billericay and I'm doing very well

I had a love affair with Nina in the back of my Cortina
a seasoned-up hyena
could not have been more obscener
she took me to the cleaners
and other misdemeanours
but I got right up between her
rum and her Ribena ...

You ask Joyce and Vicky if candy floss is sticky. I'm not a blinking thickie, I'm Billericay Dickie and I'm doing very well

I bought a lot of brandy
when I was courting Sandy
took eight to make her randy
and all I had was shandy
another thing with Sandy
what often came in handy
was passing her a mandie
she didn't half go bandy

So you ask Joyce and Vicky if I ever took the mickey. I'm not a flipping thickie, I'm Billericay Dickie and I'm doing very well

I'd a rendezvous with Janet
quite near the isle of Thanet
she looked more like a gannet
she wasn't half a prannet
her mother tried to ban it
her father helped me plan it
and when I captured Janet
she bruised her pomegranate

You ask Joyce and Vicky if I ever shaped up tricky. I'm not a blooming thickie, I'm Billericay Dickie and I'm doing very well

You should never pull the candle
if you don't know where it's been
the jackpot is in the handle
of a normal fruit machine

So you ask Joyce and Vicky who's their favourite brickie. I'm not a common thickie, I'm Billericay Dickie and I'm doing very well

I know a lovely old toerag
obliging and noblesse
kindly Charmaine Shag
from Shoeburyness
my given name is Dickie
I come from Billericay
I thought you'd never guess

You ask Joyce and Vicky, a pair of squeaky chickies. I'm not a flaming thickie, I'm Billericay Dickie and I'm doing very well

Oh golly, oh gosh
come lie on the couch
with a nice bit of posh
from Burham-on-Crouch
my given name is Dickie
I come from Billericay
and I ain't a slouch

You ask Joyce and Vicky about Billericay Dickie. I ain't an effing thickie, you ask Joyce and Vicky, I'm doing very well.

Billericay Dickie by Ian Dury and Chas Jankel, 1977
© Templemill Music Ltd/Warner-Chappell Music Ltd

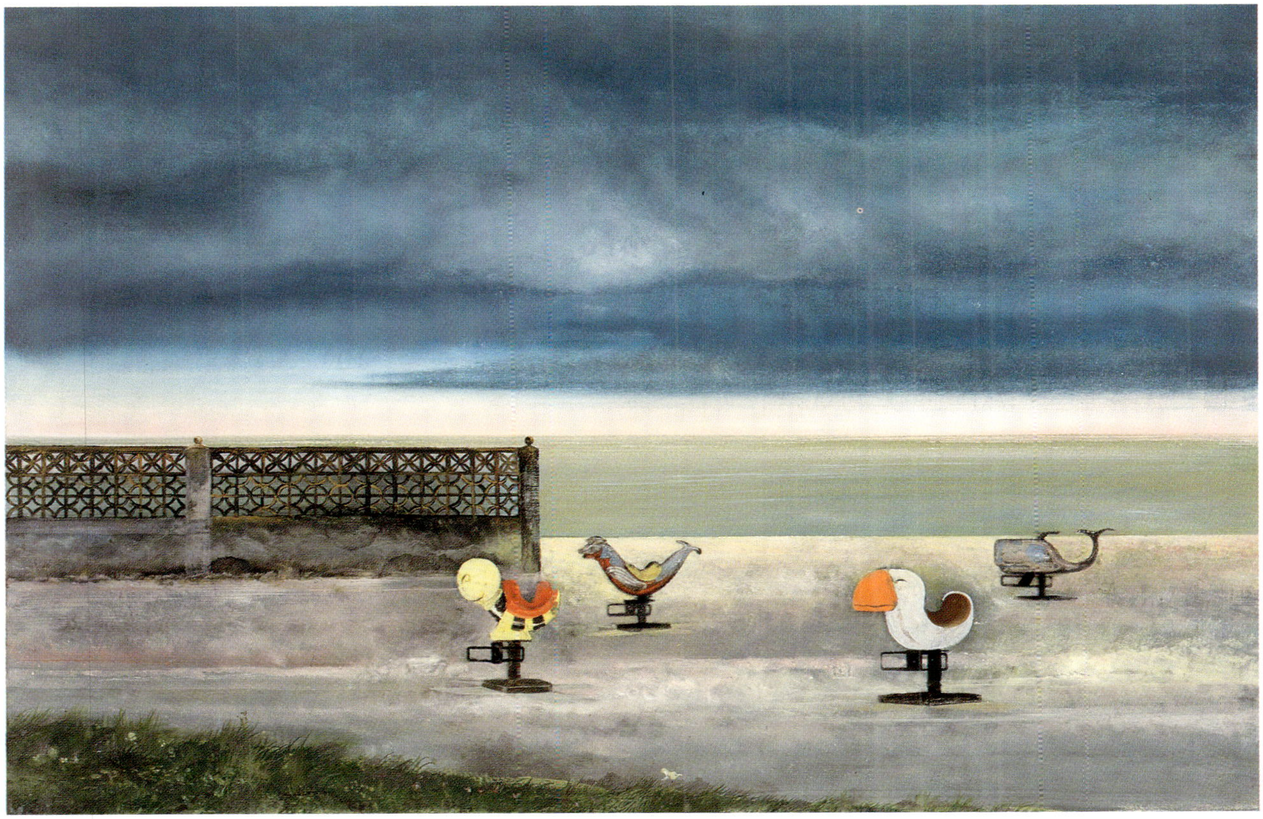

Essex, 2000, oil on canvas, 101 x 153 cm

Mary Rose Beaumont

Two Prods on Sandy Row, 1988, is a painting about a place and people seen and remembered, executed with confidence by an artist now familiar with his subject. The picture was triggered off by the sight of two boys seen from the back on their way to play snooker. They are an ill-matched couple, the one on the right looking round aggressively, as if scenting trouble, dressed quite conventionally in a jacket and trousers. The one on the left might be a little soft in the head, childishly dressed in short pants and a balaclava helmet, looking towards his companion for a lead, his face vacant and unfocused. They are framed and hemmed in by nationalist insignia: to the right a post scrawled with the letters UVF (Ulster Volunteer Force) and adorned with the Red Hand of Ulster surmounted by the beginnings of the slogan 'No Surrender'. Over their heads is a makeshift arch, topped by a naive and conventionalised statue of King William III – King Billy – and the vital dates 1690–1912. (1690 was the date of the Battle of the Boyne when the forces of the exiled King James II were defeated by those of King William of Orange, newly acceded to the English throne. In 1912 the Ulster Volunteer Force was formed; in that same year thousands of Ulstermen headed by Sir Edward Carson, leader of the Ulster Unionists, signed the sacred covenant opposing Home Rule.) Red, white and blue flags flutter round their heads like a flock of birds. The scene is a prelude to a night of violence on the 11th July, when bonfires are lit and effigies of the Pope are burned, people staying up all night chanting and drinking in the manner of a tribal ritual. On the 12th is the big Parade, which consists of scores of Pipe Bands drawn from different areas, including England and Scotland, who march and drum and throw the mace in a massive gesture of defiance and solidarity.

Extract from the catalogue essay for McFadyen's solo exhibition at Forum, Hamburg, 1989

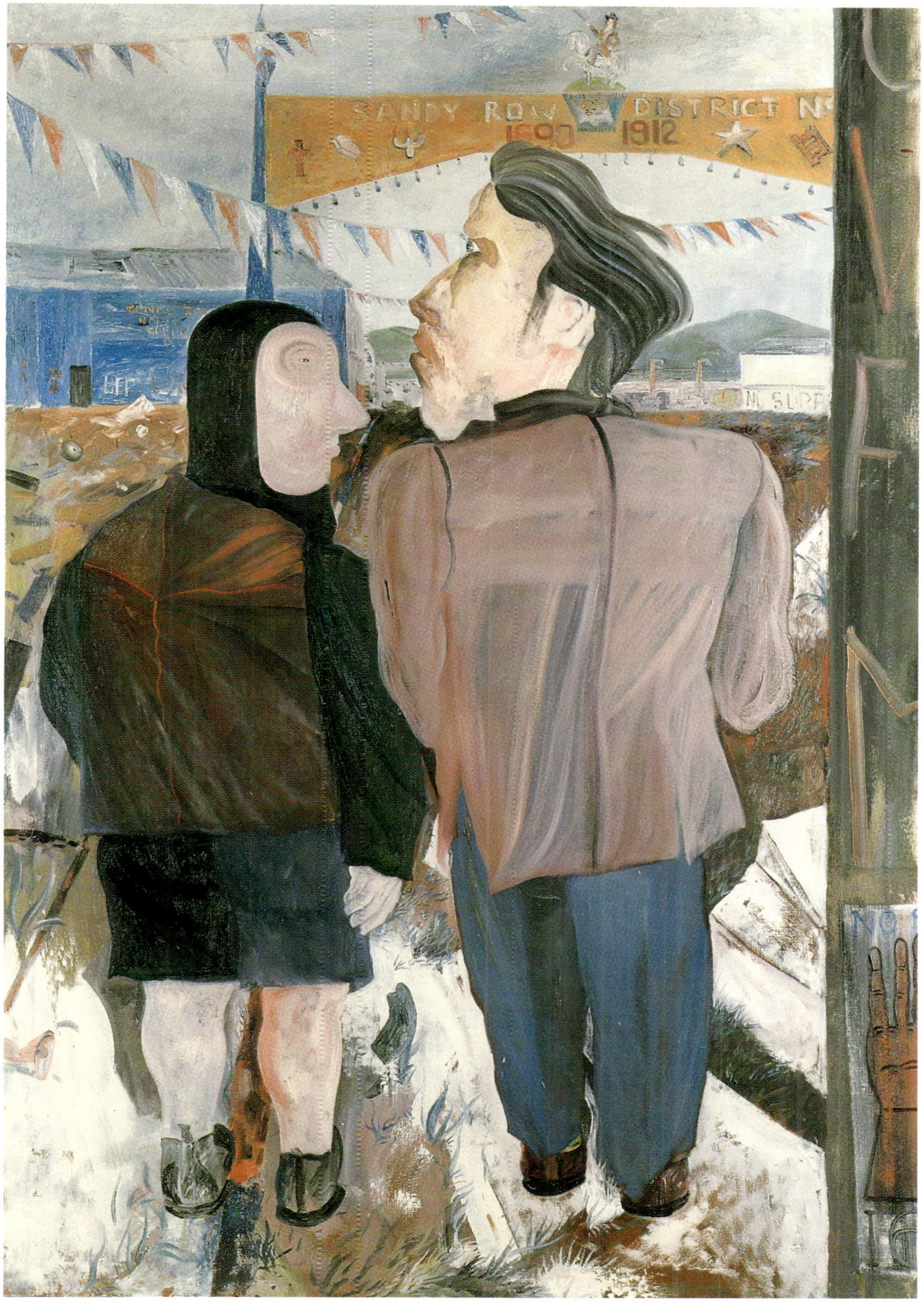

Two Prods on Sandy Row, 1988, oil on canvas, 178 x 122 cm, Private collection

Duncan Macmillan

A hundred and fifty years ago, more or less, in *The Stones of Venice*, Ruskin argued that architecture is a direct projection, not just of our physical needs, but of our whole morality. Jock McFadyen follows that lead. A Scot who has worked most of his life in London, McFadyen has made cities his study. First it was their inhabitants, but now it is the cities themselves, London especially, but recently Edinburgh too, seeking out the badly stitched seams in the cities' fabric, places for distraction, cinemas and bingo halls, edges, desolate landscapes, tube stations, intermediate places that are neither city nor countryside [...].

The shift in his work from foreground to background coincided with the commission in 1992 to design the stage sets for the Royal Ballet production of Kenneth MacMillan's ballet *The Judas Tree*. It was an opportunity to think of the background as the painting. He had always wanted to do that, concentrating on the building and leaving out the figures. But it proved not to be easy. Again he starts from photographs, and the first painting that he did of a building entirely without figures was *Mare Street Snooker Centre* in 1994. The simplicity of this facade confronting us across a street conceals the formal skill that has gone into its making. To an extent figures define their own space. Buildings pose a new kind of compositional problem, but commanding it he has created a series of monumental architectural paintings: underground stations, cinemas, blocks of flats by night, an urban railway viaduct, all encrusted with evidence of use, not just graffiti, but a whole palimpsest of signs, repairs, alterations, a surface as live as a barnacle-encrusted seaside rock pool.

Extract from *The Human Hive*, the essay for the catalogue for McFadyen's solo exhibition *Looking out to sea* at the Talbot Rice Art Gallery, Edinburgh Festival, 1998

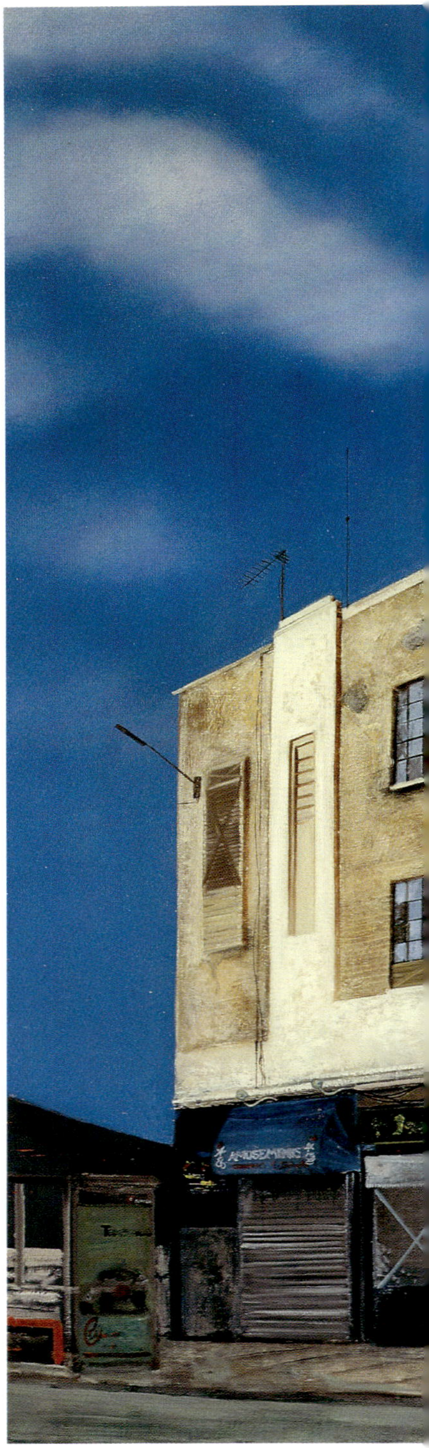

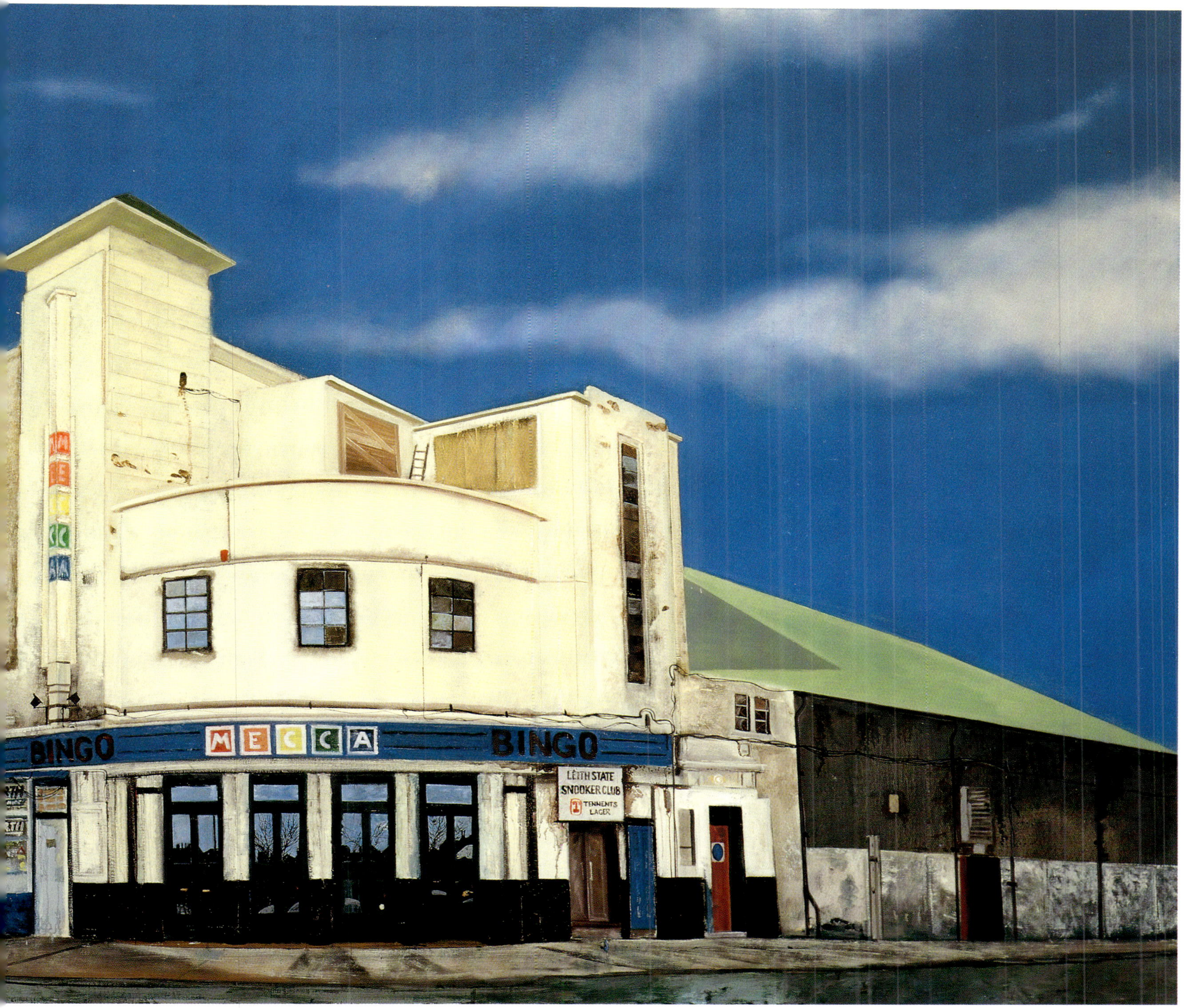

Great Junction Street, 1998, oil on canvas, 198 x 300 cm, City of Edinburgh Collection

Jeffery Camp

Beware the open eye may let things in. Scotland's Jock McFadyen escaped Slade measuring to become art erudite at Chelsea, a star resident at the National Gallery. His force, farce, pop and design made a spectacular display. Today, dry, black and bitter humour make a Céline mood. The imagination is clear. Thumbs and thumbnails are sharp in paint. East End pub regulars sweat in Jock's dreams. Jock's friend the elegant white poodle, George, sniffs out subjects, poses and manages the painter, allowing him to design the pig eyes centred in concentric rings of worn, greasy, grey pink flesh made as shapely as a well-clipped George. Mask hard. Burra hard. The flat drawing preserves the surface. Another way would be to draw solidly like Carpaccio but the scalpel wit might suffer. McFadyen looks at all art, Steinberg, Hockney, Blue Picasso, Dix, even at the harridans of Colquhoun, painty Kondracki and at the great Goya. Bacon paints the rich for the rich. His distortion achieves a shirt-tailed night club neurosis. Jock distorts for expressive art. His street marketeer cannot buy his portrait: it would cost his annual income. Imagining severe burns ulcerates thought. I keep my nerve when good and bad seem balanced. Stanley Spencer's Crucifixion is full of his own terminal pain. Grünewald's Isenheim altarpiece is pain raised to summit catharsis. Healthy Jock McFadyen looks the wall eye in the eye. His work is harsh and eloquent.

Written by the painter for the catalogue of McFadyen's solo exhibition *Canal* at the William Jackson Gallery, London, 1991

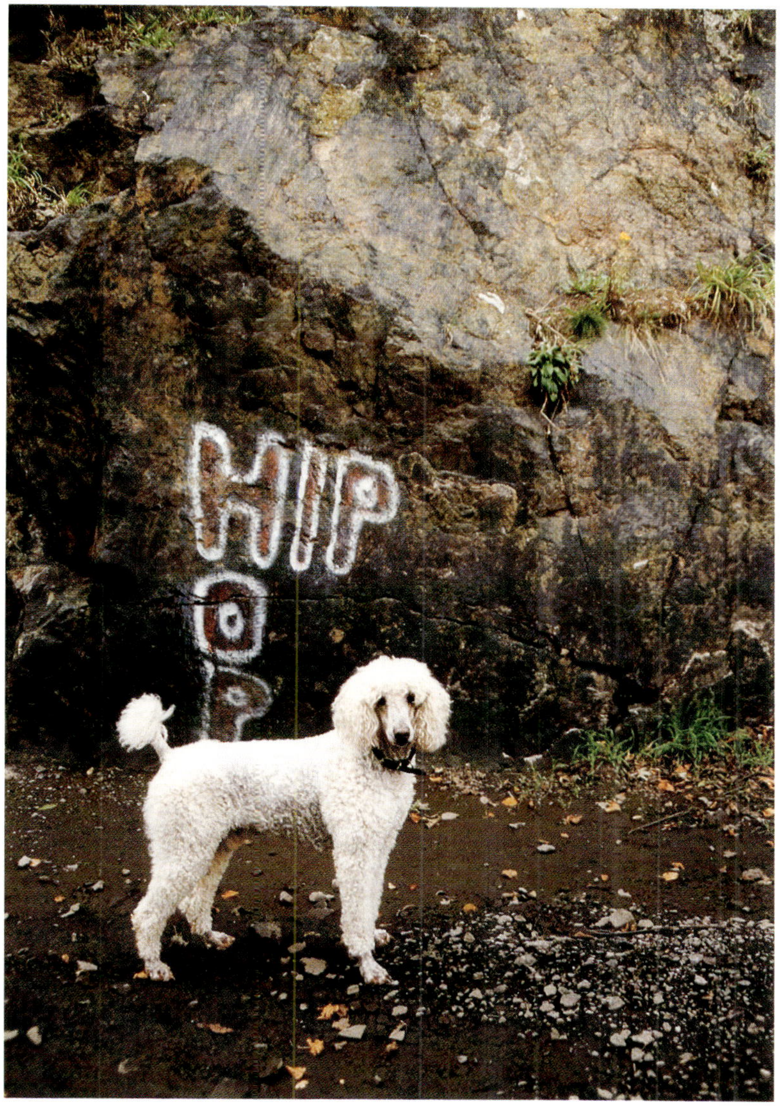

George on Calton Hill

Will Self

There's No Reggae In Orkney

'There's no reggae in Orkney', the young proprietor of Sounds in Kirkwall said, and looked up at me with mild disbelief in the afternoon fustiness of his emporium. 'There's not much call for it', he extemporised. 'We've Gaelic music of all stamps, and naturally the local traditional. There's folk – eclectic and electric; and all manners of pop and rock; there's a steady demand for classical music ... but – '

' – No reggae?'

'No reggae, no blue beat, no rock steady, no ska, no dub, no lovers', no roots – '

' – No reggae.'

'Aye – right enough; see, we'd a peedie little thing called the Human Genome Project pass through here a while ago. Now, it would appear that while the Orcadians are an ancient people, we are not – as we might wish to believe – one of the Lost Tribes of Israel; we are not as some fools say – Rastafarians; and so, you see, we have no reggae.'

No deep bass thud or strummed chop of rhythm guitar as I step out into the curiously bright gloom of a premature dusk. The lights of the tea shops opposite are strung up over displays of small iced mountains and ... many rivers to cross ... across the way, from out of a wynd comes Jimmy Cliff and he's etched for a moment against the serrated stone corner of a house, his patchwork cap, his leather jacket, his nickel-plated automatic all caught for an instant, sharply defined as plastic wrapped bags of lady struggle by together with many others leaning against the wind, like grounded gulls. Then Cliff turns and skanks back up the wynd, in the direction of the Cathedral and still there's no reggae in Orkney.

As I wheel out of Kirkwall and hammer over the shoulder of Wideford Hill, past the newspaper, past the golf club, I can hear no sounds at all save for the continuous drumskins of rubber unrolling beneath me, smitten by the endlessly lengthening sticks of tarmac. Dawning wheels around the hills and the golden mackerel sky wheels around the outer islands, and the whole tide cosmology of Orkney wheels within this: a right, tight little orrery; a lobster balanced on a salmon balanced on a cow – and still there's no reggae in Orkney, no music in this beautiful sphere.

And as I pass through Finstown and pass by the wood at Binscarth, I see ancient Rastas as old as Maeshowe – in amongst the spindly trees, their dreadlocks like great lianas, carpeting the compost floor. And around them in the painfully clear golden light of an Orkney summer's dawn, there's an inshore catch of that mackerel sky: balls and bombs of smoke which issue from their dark mouths to wheel and disperse, as I plunge on and over and down to the shores of Loch Harray.

And the wandering Jew stones wheel around the water, and the car courses along the shore, whilst the oyster catchers bend backwards to accommodate their legs. There's no reggae in Orkney, simply this divine backbeat: the shoreline lapping, the skylarks not flapping, the burial mound static and the car tyres slapping the taut way south.

To where, beyond the final ragged line of Stenness, the road mounts once more to breast Quholm; and there another breaker of darkling green swells up to encompass the flashing sea of Scapa, a great rushing tsunami of cacophonous silence, which sits solid, immutable save for coloured copings: white and silver and blue and tawny.

And in the thickening light of day I can see the *Ola* drawing into dock and I can see the cars and vans and bikes and people massing into lines, each to be engorged, each to be reborn in a lesser smaller place. I know you're on the ship, my love, and that you will come to me in room No 3 of the Stromness Hotel, so I do, and such sharp love smites me, lances through me, that in that moment at last I hear the music from across the water.

There's no reggae on Orkney – not the mainland that is, but there's plenty on Hoy. Oh yes, when push comes to shove – there's plenty on Hoy. There's a lilting then a braying saxophone which blazons forth from the Cuilags sending notes like balls of lightning down into Rackwick Bay; where, in amidst the giant lumber of rocks sits an outcropping of congas, laying down a beat as heavy as the old red sandstone itself. And atop the Knap of Trowieglen the rhythm guitarist lops the land into the lengths of time as cleanly as a spade's blade bites into peat. And down below in the dark confines of the Dwarfie Stane the eternal thrumming comes forth; the great bass susurration which is the steady pulse of Orkney reggae.

Yes, there's reggae on Hoy, my love, there's spiritual music in this protective rampart, this reclining nude – that priapic spire. At Longhope Bob Marley walks the strand, staring across to the sands on the far side of North Bay. He can feel the reggae on Hoy, the reggae in Hoy, it's no exile for Bob, my love, no exile at all.

And I'll see you walk across from the jetty my love and mount the steps to the hotel. And it will always be the fifties here my love and we'll always never have been born. And in the bar the divers drink Dark Island my love and talk of the metal below, but we can hear the reggae coming from Hoy my love, growing louder over the sound of the storm.

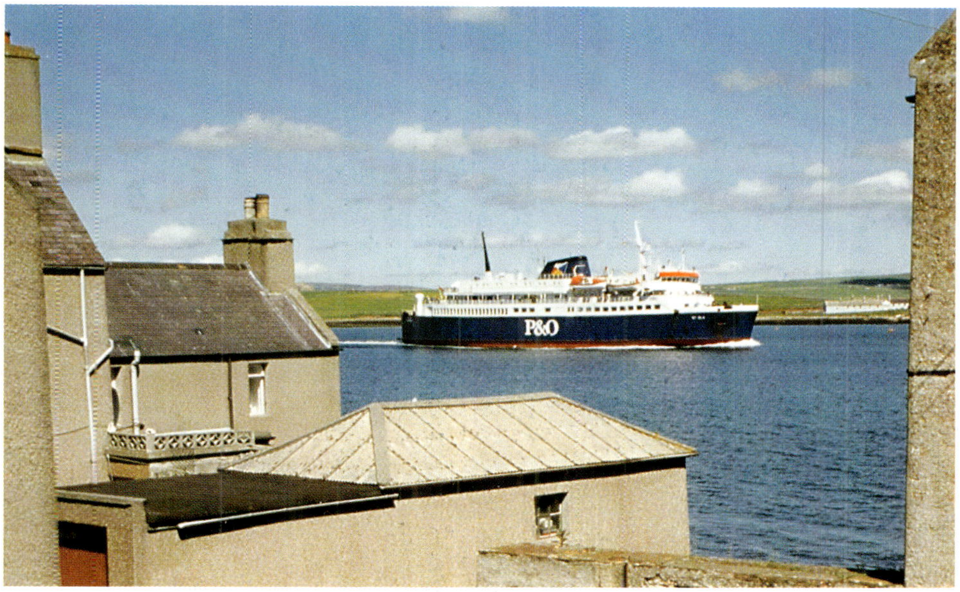

Specially written for McFadyen's solo exhibition *From Orkney and other places* at The Pier Arts Centre, Stromness, Orkney, St Magnus Festival, 1999

OVERLEAF *Hoy*, 1999, oil on canvas, 101 x 202 cm

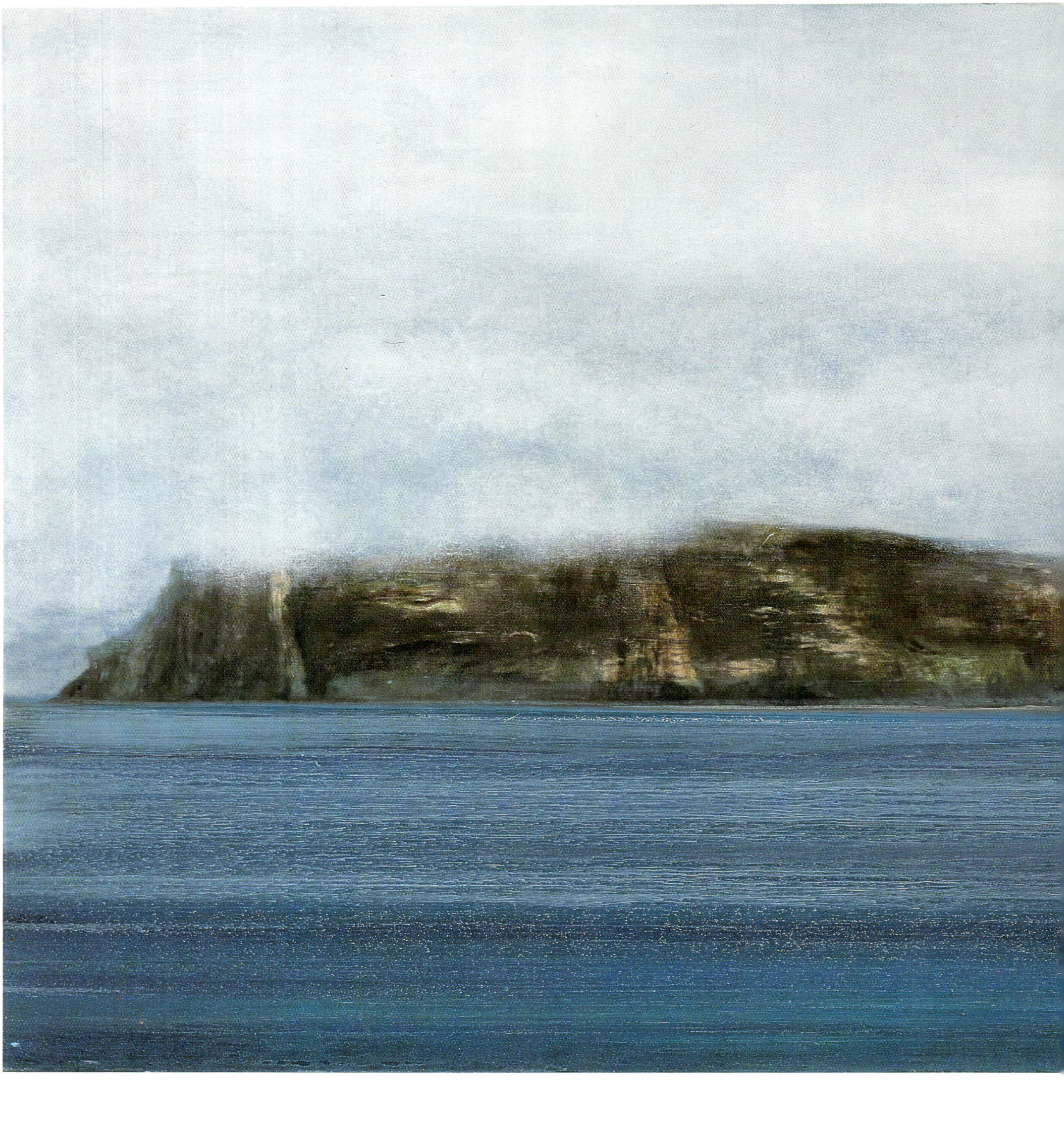

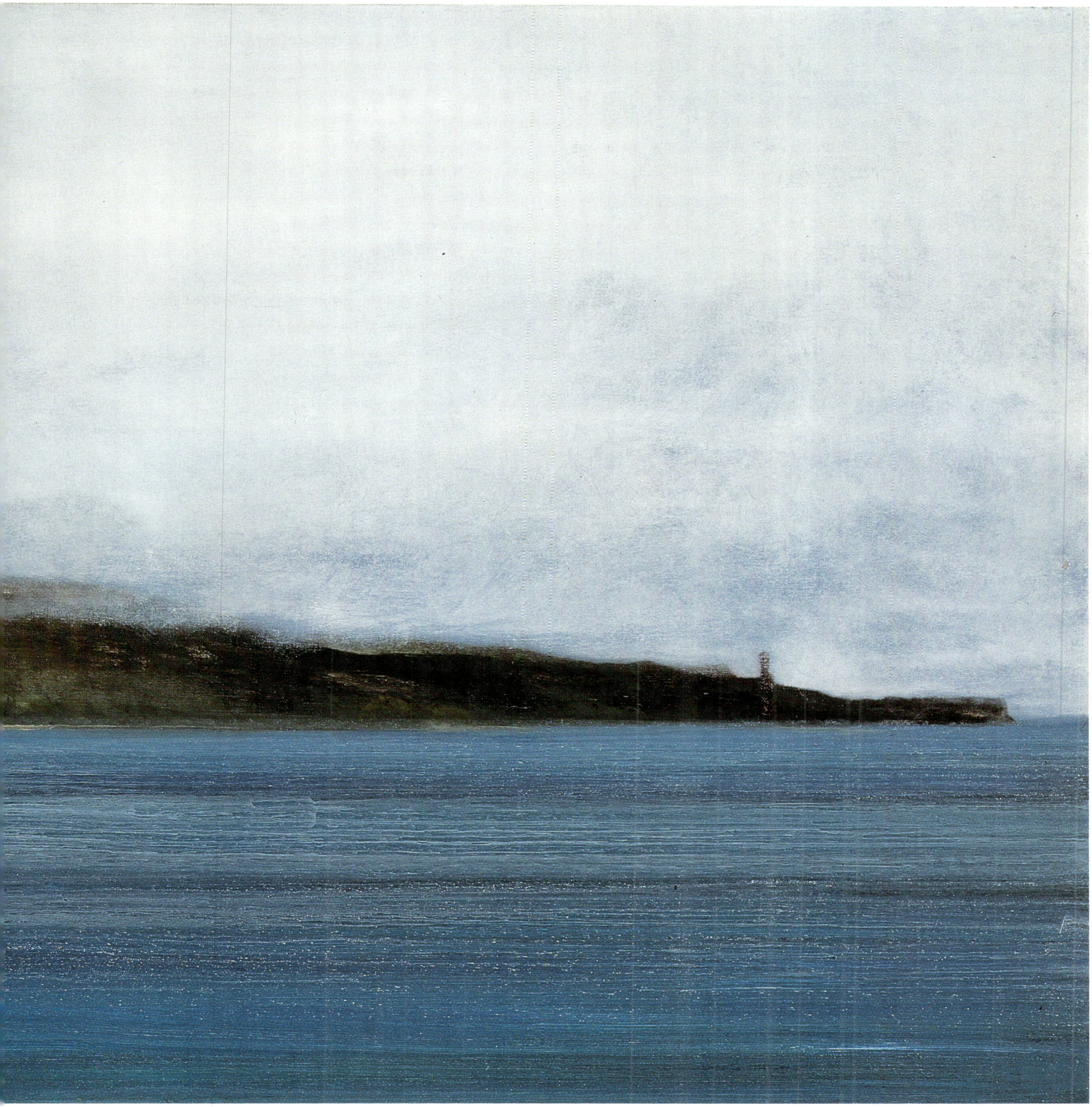

Jock McFadyen

Selected solo exhibitions

1978 Acme Gallery, London
New 57 Gallery, Edinburgh
1979 Acme Gallery, London
1980 Bede Gallery, Jarrow
1981 Blond Fine Art, London
St Paul's Gallery, Leeds
1982 Compass Gallery, Glasgow
The National Gallery, London
Blond Fine Art, London
1983 Blond Fine Art, London
1986 Blond Fine Art, London
Touring exhibition, Ceolfrith Gallery, Sunderland; Birmingham Museum and Art Gallery; Stoke-on-Trent Museum and Art Gallery; Bolton Museum and Art Gallery; Arts Council Gallery, Belfast
1988 Camden Arts Centre, London
Harris Museum and Art Gallery, Preston
1989 The Scottish Gallery, London
1991 Austin Desmond Gallery, London
William Jackson Gallery, London
The Imperial War Museum, London
1992 Kelvingrove Art Gallery, Glasgow
Manchester City Art Gallery
1994 Galleri 27, Oslo
Print Show, Flowers Graphics, London
1995 The Scottish Gallery, Edinburgh
Edinburgh Printmakers' Workshop
1996 Galleri 27, Oslo
1997 *Urbasuburba* with Humphrey Ocean, The Whitworth Art Gallery, Manchester; Ormeau Baths Gallery, Belfast
1998 Kapil Jariwala Gallery, London
Talbot Rice Gallery, Edinburgh Festival
Tegnerforbundet Galleri, Oslo
1999 The Pier Arts Centre, Orkney
2001 Agnews, London

Selected group exhibitions

1975 *New Contemporaries*, Camden Arts Centre, London
Northern Young Contemporaries, The Whitworth Art Gallery, Manchester
1977 London Film Co-op, two-man show with Willie Keddell
1978 *Tolly Cobbold Eastern Arts 2nd National Exhibition*, Fitzwilliam Museum, Cambridge, and tour
Whitechapel Open, Whitechapel Art Gallery, London
New British Avant-Garde Films, Edinburgh Film Festival
1980 *John Moores Liverpool Exhibition 12*, Walker Art Gallery, Liverpool
British Painting 1940–80, Hayward Gallery, London
1981 *Fragments against Ruin*, Arts Council touring exhibition
Artists for Nuclear Disarmament, Acme Gallery, London
Through Children's Eyes, Arts Council and Southampton City Art Gallery
1982 *Hayward Annual 1982: British Drawing*, Hayward Gallery, London
2nd International Drawing Triennale, Nürnberg
Sainsbury's Images for Today, Graves Art Gallery, Sheffield
Whitechapel Open, Whitechapel Art Gallery, London
Artist as Film-maker, National Film Theatre, London
1983 *Private Views*, Arts Council touring exhibition
Grease and Water, Edinburgh Printmakers' Workshop and Scottish Arts Council tour
53 83: Three Decades of Artists from Inner London Art Schools, Royal Academy of Arts, London
Printmaking in Scotland, The Royal Scottish Academy, Edinburgh
1984 *The Eighth British International Print Biennale*, Bradford
20th-Century Watercolours, Victoria & Albert Museum, London
The British Art Show, Arts Council touring exhibition
Amnesty International, County Hall, London, and tour
Dogworks, Interim Art, London
Whitechapel Open, Whitechapel Art Gallery, London
1985 *Artists against Apartheid*, Royal Festival Hall, London
Human Interest: Fifty Years of British Art about People, selected by Norbert Lynton, Cornerhouse, Manchester
1986 *Contrariwise*, Glyn Vivian Art Gallery, Swansea
Whitechapel Open, Whitechapel Art Gallery, London
Human Zoo, Nottingham Castle
Jock McFadyen and Steven McKenna, Contemporary Art Society Gifts, Manchester City Art Gallery
1987 *State of the Nation*, Herbert Art Gallery and Museum, Coventry
Whitechapel Open, Whitechapel Art Gallery, London
The Self Portrait: A Modern View, selected by Edward Lucie-Smith and Sean Kelly, Artsite Gallery, Bath, and tour
On a Plate, Serpentine Gallery, London
1988 *The New British Painting*, touring exhibition organised by The Contemporary Arts Center, Cincinnati, touring Chicago, Milwaukee, Winston-Salem, Grand Rapids and New York
Cries and Whispers: New Works for the British Council Collection, British Council touring exhibition
1989 *Picturing people: British Figurative Art since 1945*, British Council exhibition touring Kuala Lumpur, Hong Kong and Singapore
1990 *The Subjective City*, Cleveland Gallery, Middlesbrough
Glasgow's Great British Art Show, McLellan Galleries, Glasgow
Bellany, Howson, McFadyen, Pamela Auchincloss Gallery, New York
New British Painting, with David Tindle and Gwen Hardie, Galerie Inge Baecker, Cologne
1991 *From Bacon to Now: The Outsider in British Figuration*, Palazzo Vecchio, Florence
John Moores Liverpool Exhibition 17, prize winner, Walker Art Gallery, Liverpool
Scottish Art in the 20th Century, Royal West of England Academy, Bristol
1992 *Innocence and Experience: Images of Children in British Art from 1600 to the Present*, touring exhibition, Manchester City Art Gallery; Ferens Art Gallery, Hull; Castle Museum, Nottingham; Kelvingrove Art Gallery, Glasgow
1993 *John Moores Liverpool Exhibition 18*, Walker Art Gallery, Liverpool
1994 *Ceasefire: Reflections of Conflict by 16 British and Irish Artists*, Wolverhampton Art Gallery
1995 *30 Years of Northern Young Contemporaries*, The Whitworth Art Gallery, Manchester
1996 Inaugural exhibition of the Gallery of Modern Art, Glasgow
London Exotics, Sacy-le-Petit, Picardy, France
Wheels on Fire, Wolverhampton Art Gallery
An American Passion: The Kasen Summer Collection of British Painting, McLellan Galleries, Glasgow, and The Royal College of Art, London
The Power of Images, Martin-Gropius-Bau, Berlin
1997 *Monotypes*, with Jeffery Camp, Eileen Cooper and Michael Kane, Artspace, London
British Figurative Art Part One: Painting, Flowers East, London
1998 *British Figurative Art Part Two: Sculpture*, Flowers East, London
1999 *Contemporary British Landscape*, Flowers East, London
Scotland's Art, Festival exhibition, Edinburgh City Art Centre
20th-Century Art Birmingham Museum and Art Gallery

Selected bibliography

Exh.cat. by Jim Latter and Simon Read for solo show, New 57 Gallery, Edinburgh, 1978

Jock McFadyen: Paintings by Lewis Biggs, exh.cat., Northern Centre for Contemporary Art, solo touring exhibition, 1986

Forum by Mary Rose Beaumont, exh.cat. for solo show, Hamburg, 1989

John Bellany, Peter Howson and Jock McFadyen, by Mary Rose Beaumont, exh.cat., Pamela Auchincloss Gallery, New York, 1990

Canal, introduction by Jeffery Camp and essay by Howard Jacobson, exh.cat. for solo show, William Jackson Gallery, London, 1991

Fragments from Berlin, essay by Tom Lubbock and foreword by Angela Weight, exh.cat. for solo show, Imperial War Museum and tour, 1991

Artline, interview with Keith Patrick, Spring 1992, vol.5, no.7

Print Quarterly, 'Jock McFadyen at Paupers Press' by Robert Macdonald, 1993, vol.X, no.2

Urbasuburba with 'Island Life' by Will Self, story commissioned for exh.cat. for The Whitworth Art Gallery touring exhibition of the work of Jock McFadyen and Humphrey Ocean, 1997

Looking out to sea with 'The Human Hive', essay by Duncan Macmillan, exh.cat. for solo exhibition, Talbot Rice Art Gallery, Edinburgh Festival, 1998

From Orkney and other places, 'There's no reggae in Orkney', story by Will Self, exh.pub. commissioned for solo exhibition, Pier Arts Centre, Orkney, 1999

Selected television

1979	BBC2, documentary on the Arts Council (including an interview with Jock McFadyen)
1982	STV, documentary feature
	Channel 4, *Alter Image* feature
1988	BBC2, *Review* feature on McFadyen's solo show at Camden Arts Centre
	LWT, *South of Watford* feature
	Channel 4, *The Self Portrait* feature
1989	Channel 4, *Box Office*
1990	Channel 4, Mentorn Films, *52*, television project
1991	Channel 4, *Box Office*
1992	Channel 4, *Box Office*
1997	Channel 4, *The Judas Tree*

Radio

Many radio contributions including *World at One*, *Kaleidoscope*, *Night Waves and Third Ear*, thirty minute interview on the artist's work with William Feaver, Radio 3, 1991

Awards/ commissions

1978	Arts Council Award for film-making project
1979	Arts Council Major Award
1981	Artist in Residence at the National Gallery, London
1991	Prize winner John Moores Liverpool Exhibition 17
1992	Designed sets and costumes for Kenneth MacMillan's ballet *The Judas Tree*, Royal Opera House, Covent Garden

Public collections

Amnesty International
Arts Council of Great Britain
BBC
Bede Gallery, Jarrow
Birmingham Museum and Art Gallery
British Council
British Museum
City of Edinburgh
Cleveland Gallery, Middlesbrough
Contemporary Art Society
Glasgow Art Galleries
The Government Art Collection
The Guildhall, London
Hunterian Art Gallery, Glasgow
The Imperial War Museum, London
Kunsthalle, Hamburg
Leicester Education Authority
Lillie Art Gallery, Glasgow
Manchester City Art Gallery
The Museum of London
The National Gallery, London
Scottish Arts Council
Sheffield City Art Gallery
The Theatre Museum, London
Walsall Museum and Art Gallery
The Whitworth Art Gallery, Manchester
Wolverhampton Art Gallery
Worcester Art Gallery

Jock McFadyen was born in Paisley in 1950.
He studied at Chelsea School of Art (BA 1976 and MA 1977).
He lives and works in London.

OVERLEAF *Sleeping Man*, 1995, oil on canvas, 60 x 76 cm

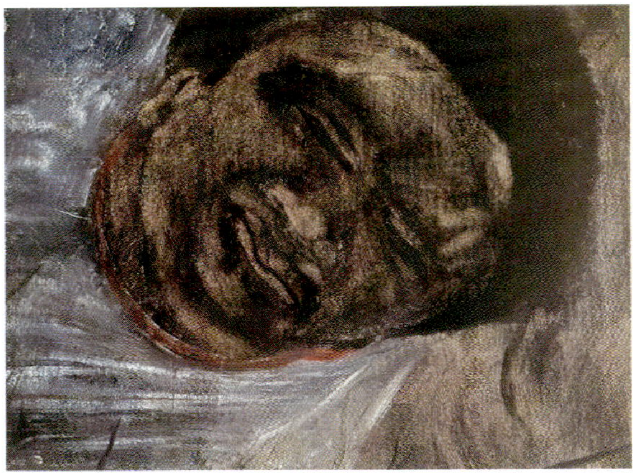

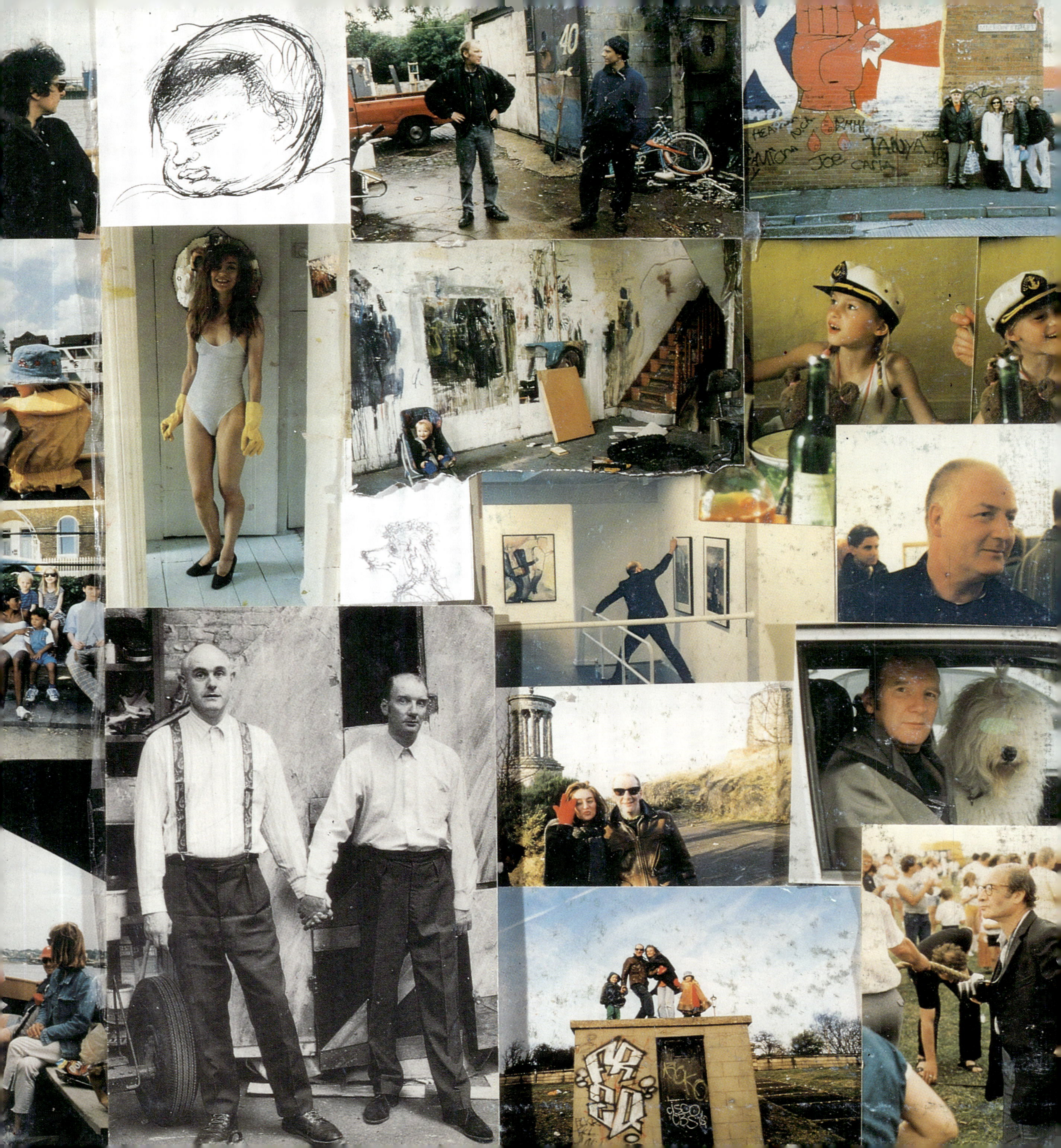
40
TANYA
JOE